Commanded in All Things

Robert Smith

March 2, 2014

"I will delight myself in thy statutes: I will not forget thy word."
–Psalm 119:16

Contents

CONTENTS

From the Throne of God

"...which is the law by which all things are governed,
even the power of God who sitteth upon his throne,
who is in the bosom of eternity, who is in the midst of
all things."

–D&C 88:13

The LDS endowment ceremony teaches us the preeminence of God's word. It is God's word that causes the organization of our world,[1] as well as all things that occupy it. It is God's word that causes a man's sins to be forgiven. It is obedience to God's word that sanctifies man. It is God's word that brings a man back into God's presence.

Throughout the endowment, we are exposed to a system for the distribution of God's word. We see Heavenly Father speaking to Jesus Christ. We see Jesus Christ speaking to angels. We see

---

[1] "And I, God, called the light Day; and the darkness, I called Night; and this I did by the word of my power, and it was done as I spake; and the evening and the morning were the first day." (Moses 2:5)

5

angels speaking to men. Through each messenger, the word of God remains true to its original content. Neither Jesus nor his angels add to, take away from, or modify the message they receive. There is not an individual in that series who is authorized to remove from, alter, or invent, even when the chain is augmented by adding a final link of a human messenger. Were removal, modification, or invention to occur, the changed portion would cease to be God's word and there would be no power in it. All happiness is found in the word of God.[2]

The Lord commands us to heed his word:

> And I give unto you a commandment, that ye shall forsake all evil and cleave unto all good, that ye shall live by every word which proceedeth forth out of the mouth of God. (D&C 98:11)

It is exceedingly important for us to obey this commandment. After all, the righteous are not those who profess a particular creed or are members of a particular culture, but those who serve God.[3] To serve God, one must seek, discern, and heed his word. Understanding the origin of God's word, where we receive it from,

---

[2] "And now, Zerahemnah, I command you, in the name of that all-powerful God, who has strengthened our arms that we have gained power over you, by our faith, by our religion, and by our rites of worship, and by our church, and by the sacred support which we owe to our wives and our children, by that liberty which binds us to our lands and our country; yea, and also by the maintenance of the sacred word of God, to which we owe all our happiness; and by all that is most dear unto us." (Alma 44:5)

[3] See Malachi 3:18

and how we receive it is essential to being counted among the righteous. This chapter explores just how the word proceeds forth from the mouth of God.

Jesus Christ

The first few verses of John in the King James Bible read,

> In the beginning was the Word, and the Word was with God, and the Word was God. The same was in the beginning with God. All things were made by him; and without him was not any thing made that was made. (John 1:1-3)

The Inspired Version reads:

> In the beginning was the gospel preached through the Son. And the gospel was the word, and the word was with the Son, and the Son was with God, and the Son was of God. The same was in the beginning with God. All things were made by him; and without him was not anything made which was made. In him was the gospel, and the gospel was the life, and the life was the light of men; (John 1:1-4, Inspired Version)

There is an alternate translation that reads, "in the ruling council there was a spokesman, and the spokesman was among the gods, and the spokesman was a god."[4]

---

[4]This translation is purported to be by Hugh Nibley; however I can't find a source.

7

The concept of Jesus Christ as God's messenger is in accordance with what we know through Joseph's revelations about the premortal council of the gods.

> I shall comment on the very first Hebrew word in the Bible....It read first, "The head one of the Gods brought forth the Gods." That is the true meaning of the words....In the beginning, the head of the Gods called a council of the Gods; and they came together and concocted a plan to create the world and people it. (TPJS, p. 349)

John described the Savior's role by saying:

> And he bore record, saying: I saw his glory, that he was in the beginning, before the world was; Therefore, in the beginning the Word was, for he was the Word, even the messenger of salvation— The light and the Redeemer of the world; the Spirit of truth, who came into the world, because the world was made by him, and in him was the life of men and the light of men. (D&C 93:7-9)

All of these scriptures teach us that Jesus Christ is the spokesperson for Heavenly Father. With exceedingly few exceptions,[5] most of the recorded words of the Father in the scriptures came through Christ. Significantly, the Father calls the Son the word of his power: "And by the word of my power, have I created them, which is mine

---

[5]Such as when Heavenly Father testifies of his son.

Only Begotten Son, who is full of grace and truth."[6] All of God's power that we experience is a result of his word flowing through Jesus Christ.

Man can come to the point where he receives God's word directly from Christ face to face as Moses did. He can come to the point where he walks with Christ as Enoch did. This point is always preceded by the occasional receipt of the voice of Christ. The scriptures are full of examples of Jesus dispensing the word of Heavenly Father to end recipients such as Joseph Smith and his associates, the brother of Jared, Moses, Enoch, and many many others. However, not all of God's word is delivered to the end recipient directly through Christ. The purpose of the Holy Ghost, angels, and human messengers is to bring a man to the point where he can converse with Jesus face to face. Until then, Jesus dispenses his word through the Holy Ghost, angels and men.

Angels

Christ has charge over the angels. He assigns them to send his words forth to men.

> And now, he imparteth his word by angels unto men, yea, not only men but women also. Now this is not all; little children do have words given unto them many times, which confound the wise and the learned. (Alma 32:23)

> And the office of their ministry is to call men unto

---

[6]Moses 1:32

9

repentance, and to fulfill and to do the work of the covenants of the Father, which he hath made unto the children of men, to prepare the way among the children of men, by declaring the word of Christ unto the chosen vessels of the Lord, that they may bear testimony of him. (Moroni 7:31)

In scriptural instances where God has shown people his throne, we have the common description of the throne being surrounded by angels. Lehi says that God's throne is surrounded by "numberless concourses of angels in the attitude of singing and praising their God."[7] Alma Jr.'s description of the throne concurs with Lehi's: "I saw, even as our father Lehi saw, God sitting upon his throne, surrounded with numberless concourses of angels..."[8]. John also describes angels surrounding the throne.[9] These are the agents of transmission of God's word from Christ to men.

Recipients of angels do not need to have any church office or responsibility. The people of Lamoni's court—common folks in both the ecclesiastic as well as civic sense—saw angels and conversed with them, and were taught things of God (see Alma 19:34). Prisoners in jail with Nephi and Lehi also were taught by angels (see Helaman 5:48). Women and children can receive angels just as readily as men: "And now, he imparteth his word by angels unto men, yea, not only men but women also." (Alma 32:23).

As God's words do not cease, God's angels do not cease to minister. "And because he hath done this, my beloved brethren,

---

[7] 1 Nephi 1:8
[8] Alma 36:22
[9] Revelation 4:4-5

have miracles ceased? Behold I say unto you, Nay; neither have angels ceased to minister unto the children of men."[10] Angels are just as vital to the transmittence of God's word today as they ever have been.

Holy Ghost

The word of the Lord comes to men by the Holy Ghost.[11] Nephi taught that "Angels speak by the power of the Holy Ghost; wherefore, they speak the words of Christ. Wherefore, I said unto you, feast upon the words of Christ; for behold, the words of Christ will tell you all things what ye should do."[12] There is much to this verse. Does the power of the Holy Ghost give angels what to say, such as it does when a preacher is preaching by the Holy Ghost? In other words, is it the medium by which the words of Christ flow to the recipient through the angel, like a straw is the means whereby liquid travels into the mouth of the user? Or, is it the means by which the individual receives the words of Christ delivered by an angel, just as we receive mortal communications through our eyes or ears? There are scriptures that support both applications.

Moroni teaches that the Lord intends for the content of meetings in the church to be indicated by the power of the Holy

---

[10] Moroni 7:29

[11] Mormon writes: "For immediately after I had learned these things of you I inquired of the Lord concerning the matter. And the word of the Lord came to me by the power of the Holy Ghost..." (Moroni 8:7)

[12] 2 Nephi 32:3

Ghost.[13] In this sense, the power of the Holy Ghost is able to tell you what to say or do. Therefore, if angels speak by the power of the Holy Ghost, they are told what to say via the Holy Ghost.

Nephi says that "when a man speaketh by the power of the Holy Ghost the power of the Holy Ghost carrieth it unto the hearts of the children of men."[14] Therefore, the Holy Ghost can be the medium of delivery from the angel to the man.

Nephi also tells us that it was through the power of the Holy Ghost that he received his visions.

> And it came to pass after I, Nephi, having heard all the words of my father...I, Nephi, was desirous also that I might see, and hear, and know of these things, by the power of the Holy Ghost, which is the gift of God unto all those who diligently seek him, as well in times of old as in the time that he should manifest himself unto the children of men. (1 Nephi 10:17)

His visions were seen not with his mortal eyes, but with his spritual eyes. It was received by the Holy Ghost within him.

The Holy Ghost is the mind of God. "Not a desire, act, wish, or thought does the Holy Ghost indulge in contrary to that which is dictated by the Father."[15] As symbolically presented in the

---

[13] "And their meetings were conducted by the church after the manner of the workings of the Spirit, and by the power of the Holy Ghost; for as the power of the Holy Ghost led them whether to preach, or to exhort, or to pray, or to supplicate, or to sing, even so it was done." (Moroni 6:9)

[14] 2 Nephi 33:1

[15] Brigham Young, JD 6:95

endowment ceremony, the Lord, through his mind—the spirit of God—transmits messages to and through angels into the spirits of the recipients. Sometimes these messengers are visible, and sometimes they are not. Sometimes they are heard, and sometimes they are felt. Sometimes they come when the recipient is awake, and sometimes when the recipient is asleep. Many times, recipients are not able to receive angels, and so God amply puts to use human messengers.

Man

During his mortal ministry, Jesus provided the perfect example of a righteous mortal messenger of God's word. Of his message he said, "the word which ye hear is not mine, but the Father's which sent me."[16] God transmits his word through Christ to angels to true messengers. The message is always limited to God's word.

John was also a messenger. In his vision,

> ...the voice which I heard from heaven spake unto me again, and said, Go and take the little book which is open in the hand of the angel which standeth upon the sea and upon the earth. And I went unto the angel, and said unto him, Give me the little book. And he said unto me, Take it, and eat it up....And I took the little book out of the angel's hand, and ate it up...And he said unto me, Thou must prophesy again before many peoples, and nations, and tongues, and kings. (Revelation 10:8-11)

[16]John 14:24, see also John 14:23

John delivered God's words as they were delivered to him. John understood that, as Joseph Smith taught, "God will not acknowledge that which He has not called, ordained, and chosen."[17]

Ezekiel saw the throne and was told by God: "Moreover he said unto me, Son of man, eat that thou findest; eat this roll, and go speak unto the house of Israel. So I opened my mouth, and he caused me to eat that roll."[18] God delivered to Ezekiel all the words that he wanted Ezekiel to say to Israel. Ezekiel was not authorized to speak his mind, nor improvise. If he had, all those words which were his own would have fallen to the earth null and void. However, because Ezekiel was given God's word, he could be assured that God's authority backed his words. He was a messenger.

Every true messenger in scripture was commanded by God to give a set message—from Samuel the Lamanite and King Benjamin, whose message was given by angels, to the Savior himself, who spoke only what Heavenly Father told him to speak.

Conclusion

Jesus taught that he is the true vine. He is the root that connects us to the Father. Without him, we are nothing.

> I am the true vine, and my Father is the husbandman. Every branch in me that beareth not fruit he taketh away: and every branch that beareth fruit, he purgeth it, that it may bring forth more fruit. Now ye are

---

[17]HC 4:208
[18]Ezekiel 3:1-2

clean through th.
Abide in me, and .
fruit of itself, excep
ye, except ye abide 1.
branches: He that abi
same bringeth forth muc
do nothing. If a man abic
as a branch, and is wither
and cast them into the fire, a.
15:1-6)

The nutrients of a vine flow from its ro
from God's word through Christ. Inasi.
accept that word, we are grafted into the
him; we bear the fruits of his word. Hov
do not seek and accept his word, we becom.
nourishment. Here Jesus alludes to the time w.
not made a sure connection with God througl
gathered by the angels and burned.[20] As Jesus sta
word of God, we are nothing. This is because ever\
has to come as a result of the acceptation of word.
from God's throne through some combination of C.
and men to the recipient. Most are aware that salvatio.

---

[19] "That they might not be hardened against the word,
might not be unbelieving, and go on to destruction, but th.
might receive the word with joy, and as a branch be grafte.
the true vine, that they might enter into the rest of the Lord
God." (Alma 16:17)

[20] See Malachi 4:1, D&C 38:12, D&C 64:24, D&C 86:7, D&
88:94, and D&C 133:64, among others.

hrist's word, but how many realize that anything
e past his coming must also be by his word, or it
en and destroyed"?[21]

to give pause to these subjects, perhaps among the
nt in the gospel. Treating lightly God's word, which
ludes misunderstanding what it is and what it isn't,
ed by Nephi as trampling God under our feet.[22] The
ed not receiving his voice with being under the bondage

d by this you may know they are under the bondage
sin, because they come not unto me. For whoso
meth not unto me is under the bondage of sin. And
hoso receiveth not my voice is not acquainted with
my voice, and is not of me. And by this you may
know the righteous from the wicked, and that the

'I am the Lord thy God; and I give unto you this command-
t—that no man shall come unto the Father but by me or by
word, which is my law, saith the Lord. And everything that is
the world, whether it be ordained of men, by thrones, or prin-
palities, or powers, or things of name, whatsoever they may be,
at are not by me or by my word, saith the Lord, shall be thrown
down, and shall not remain after men are dead, neither in nor
after the resurrection, saith the Lord your God. For whatsoever
things remain are by me; and whatsoever things are not by me
shall be shaken and destroyed." (D&C 132:12-14)

[22] "For the things which some men esteem to be of great worth,
both to the body and soul, others set at naught and trample under
their feet. Yea, even the very God of Israel do men trample under
their feet; I would speak in other words—they set him at naught,
and hearken not to the voice of his counsels." (1 Nephi 19:7)

whole world groaneth under sin and darkness even now. (D&C 84:50-53)

This condition, God said, is due to "treating lightly the things [we] have received."[23] Thus we read the admonition of Jacob:

Behold, great and marvelous are the works of the Lord. How unsearchable are the depths of the mysteries of him; and it is impossible that man should find out all his ways. And no man knoweth of his ways save it be revealed unto him; wherefore, brethren, despise not the revelations of God. For behold, by the power of his word man came upon the face of the earth, which earth was created by the power of his word. Wherefore, if God being able to speak and the world was, and to speak and man was created, O then, why not able to command the earth, or the workmanship of his hands upon the face of it, according to his will and pleasure? Wherefore, brethren, seek not to counsel the Lord, but to take counsel from his hand. For behold, ye yourselves know that he counseleth in wisdom, and in justice, and in great mercy, over all his works. (Jacob 4:8-10)

Jacob reminds us that God has all power, that his word is the device of his power, and that revelation is the means appointed to receive his word. He suggests that the logical conclusion of an understanding of these facts is to seek and heed God's word. The

---

[23]D&C 84:54

rest of the book is dedicated to the same purpose as Jacob's. I sincerely hope it is of service to you in your journey back to God.

By Me or By My Servants

"What I the Lord have spoken, I have spoken, and I
excuse not myself; and though the heavens and the
earth pass away, my word shall not pass away, but
shall all be fulfilled, whether by mine own voice or by
the voice of my servants, it is the same."

–D&C 1:38

The Lord has commanded that we "shall live by every word
that proceedeth forth from the mouth of God."[1] As laid out in
another chapter of this book, God speaks his word to us through
his own presence, his voice, angels, and sometimes even men. We
are told that,

> ...whatsoever [the Elders of the church] shall speak
> when moved upon by the Holy Ghost shall be scripture,
> shall be the will of the Lord, shall be the mind of the
> Lord, shall be the word of the Lord, shall be the voice

---

[1]D&C 84:44

of the Lord, and the power of God unto salvation. (D&C 68:4)

An example of this principle is given by Mormon's seeking the word of God in relation to whether or not infants should be baptized. He seeks the Lord and obtains the word of God in a writable response:

> Listen to the words of Christ, your Redeemer, your Lord and your God. Behold, I came into the world not to call the righteous but sinners to repentance; the whole need no physician, but they that are sick; where-fore, little children are whole, for they are not capable of committing sin; wherefore the curse of Adam is taken from them in me, that it hath no power over them; and the law of circumcision is done away in me. And after this manner did the Holy Ghost manifest the word of God unto me; wherefore, my beloved son, I know that it is solemn mockery before God, that ye should baptize little children. (Moroni 8:9)

Several important factors are worth pointing out here. First, Mormon says that the source of this revelation was not a personal visit of Christ, but the Holy Ghost. The still small voice, in other words, is actually a voice; an audible, transcribable voice. This is consistent with how Joseph described the still small voice: "Yea, thus saith the still small voice, which whispereth through and pierceth all things, and often times it maketh my bones to quake while it maketh manifest, saying..."[2] He then goes on to give

---

[2]D&C 85:6

a lengthy "thus saith the Lord" revelation. <u>Since the word of</u> <u>God is the word that God speaks</u>, it must necessarily come via a "<u>thus saith the Lord</u>" revelation. Now, often revelation comes in a flash of intelligence that must be put to words by the recipient. However, the vital point is that <u>there is transcribable substance to</u> <u>true revelation</u>—not just emotion. It need not be long—an answer to a question of yes or no is certainly the word of God and is a single word revelation.

When the Elders (or whoever else) are speaking, the mind of the Lord, the word of the Lord, the voice of the Lord, and power unto salvation are only present inasmuch as their words are actually given to them by God. If God is speaking to them via the Holy Ghost and they repeat those words given to them, they are speaking the mind of the Lord. However, *D&C 68:4 does not mean* *that whatever a holder of church office says is God's mind*; man cannot <u>dictate the mind of God</u>. The word of God must actually come from God!

We can understand this further by analyzing the first section of the Doctrine and Covenants. Here we encounter verse 38, usually quoted without the rest of the section:

> What I the Lord have spoken, I have spoken, and I excuse not myself; and though the heavens and the earth pass away, my word shall not pass away, but shall all be fulfilled, whether by mine own voice or by the voice of my servants, it is the same.

As we have shown elsewhere in this book, <u>in order for words</u> <u>to have the power of God, they must proceed from the throne</u>

down, not from earth up. Therefore, taken in conjunction with what God said elsewhere in the scriptures, the Lord can only be saying here, "if someone speaks the words of God, it doesn't matter whether that someone is me or someone else, I will own those words, because they came from me." Note that this is not the same as saying, "whatever a church office holder says, I will consider that as if I had said it, even though the words did not come from me." He explicitly says "what *I* have spoken." In fact, he says it twice. The "whether by mine own voice" is not variable in the source of the word, but only variable in terms of which messenger (the Lord himself, an angel, or a man) delivered it. The word "servant" here does not indicate an office, but simply a role that can as easily be filled by a child[3] as a patriarch, or a heathen as a saint. The only qualification for a true messenger is that the word they carry, as brief as it may be, originates from God. It is supremely important to heed God's word no matter who the messenger may be.

> And wo be unto him that will not hearken unto the words of Jesus, and also to them whom *he hath chosen and sent among them*; for whoso receiveth not *the words of Jesus and the words of those whom he hath sent* receiveth not him; and therefore he will not receive them at the last day; (3 Nephi 28:34)

---

[3] "And now, he imparteth his word by angels unto men, yea, not only men but women also. Now this is not all; little children do have words given unto them many times, which confound the wise and the learned." (Alma 32:23)

Messengers of God can be a motley crew. On the one hand, we see that Caiaphas' role as a messenger of God was not abrogated despite his being guilty of the blood of Christ, for it was he who prophesied (or, in other words, spoke God's word) that it were better that one man die than a nation. On the other hand, we see Jesus of Nazareth, not only void of church authority or office, but also grossly unorthodox, whose only credential was that his message actually came from God. He did not use any other signet of authority besides simply claiming that his message was from God. He said, "He that loveth me not keepeth not my sayings: and the word which ye hear is not mine, but the Father's which sent me."[4] Even to the Nephites, to whom he appeared in resurrected glory and in plain display of his divinity, his authority was simply as the messenger of the Father, come to deliver his word:

> Behold I have given unto you my gospel, and this is the gospel which I have given unto you—that I came into the world to do the will of my Father, *because my Father sent me*...And this is the word which he hath given unto the children of men. And for this cause he fulfilleth *the words which he hath given*, and he lieth not, but fulfilleth all his words. (3 Nephi 27:13,18)

Interestingly, like Abinadi, John the Baptist, Lehi, and the majority of scriptural prophets, Jesus' message was from God and supremely official despite his never having been appointed by the duly recognized authorities nor sustained by the body of the church. This did not invalidate the source of his message nor

---

[4]John 14:24

23

nullify God's word as preached through him.

The origination from God is critically important. Even Joseph, whose words God commanded us to receive as his own (an endorsement I am not aware of any other man having received in this dispensation), had a limitation placed in his endorsement. God explicitly limits his commission as a messenger to his word: "Wherefore, meaning the church, thou shalt give heed unto all his words and commandments which he shall give unto you *as he receiveth them*, walking in all holiness before me;"[5] Thus we call these people messengers and not, say, authors. No man can dictate God's word independent of God giving it to him.

Because messengers are only true when their message emanates from God, true messengers always plainly identify the heavenly source of their message. Nephi son of Helaman "declare[d] unto them the word of the Lord which had been spoken unto him."[6] Jesus commanded the Nephite twelve to "declare the words which I have spoken, unto the ends of the earth."[7] He told Abraham, "I show these things unto thee before ye go into Egypt, that ye may declare all these words."[8] Enoch saw a vision where "the Lord spake with me, and gave me commandment" to speak specific words to specific people.[9] King Benjamin's famous speech was an exposition of "the words which had been delivered unto him by the angel of the Lord" the night before.[10] Jacob spoke on the

---

[5]D&C 21:4
[6]Helaman 10:12
[7]3 Nephi 11:41
[8]Abraham 3:15
[9]Moses 6:42
[10]Mosiah 4:1

errand of the Lord, who explicitly gave him the words to say:

> Wherefore, I must tell you the truth according to the plainness of the word of God. For behold, as I inquired of the Lord, thus came the word unto me, saying: Jacob, get thou up into the temple on the morrow, and declare the word which I shall give thee unto this people. (Jacob 2:11)

He said, "Do not say that I have spoken hard things against you; for if ye do, ye will revile against the truth; for I have spoken the words of your Maker."[11] His brother Nephi similarly received the text of his sermons not only from his encounters with angels but from the "words of [his] Maker"[12]:

> And if they are not the words of Christ, judge ye—for Christ will show unto you, with power and great glory, that they are his words, at the last day; and you and I shall stand face to face before his bar; and ye shall know that I have been commanded of him to write these things, notwithstanding my weakness. (2 Nephi 33:11)

Alma Jr. tells us that his father and Abinadi both spoke the words that were given them from God:

> Behold, I can tell you—did not my father Alma believe in the words which were delivered by the mouth of

---

[11]2 Nephi 9:40
[12]2 Nephi 33:11

Abinadi? And was he not a holy prophet? Did he not speak the words of God, and my father Alma believe them? (Alma 5:11)

The foregoing personalities are the most powerful preachers in scripture. If they (including the Savior) would not pretend to preach the gospel except God dispensed his word to them, should we? God said,

> Seek not to declare my word, but first seek to obtain my word, and then shall your tongue be loosed; then, if you desire, you shall have my Spirit and my word, yea, the power of God unto the convincing of men. (D&C 11:21)

He has told us that we need to treasure his word up in our minds in order to be blessed to be given his words when the necessity arises:

> Neither take ye thought beforehand what ye shall say; but treasure up in your minds continually the words of life, and it shall be given you in the very hour that portion that shall be meted unto every man. (D&C 84:85)

Note that the phrase "every man" seems to indicate that this command is to every man, not just those who are wont to have spiritual experiences. God makes this explicit by explaining that those who preach are only to do so by (or in accordance with or through the means of) the Comforter, thus giving them God's word.[13] Joseph said the same: "All are to preach the Gospel, by the power and influence of the Holy Ghost; and no man can preach the Gospel without the Holy Ghost."[14] "If ye receive not the Spirit ye shall not teach."[15] God has commanded us to declare *his* word, not our own: "And in this place let them lift up their voice and declare *my* word with loud voices..."[16]

And what of those who do not preach God's word but teach by "some other way?" All the pretense of a false messenger is worthless if the individual does not, in fact, possess a message from the throne of God. For all his office, King Noah and the like never delivered the word of God. Abinadi tells us that though King Noah's priests considered themselves teachers over the people and knew at least a few verses, they failed to teach the people even the simplest saving doctrines, and were woefully ignorant of the gospel. The church office of Noah and his priests (who had been duly ordained by those who had authority and were sustained by their people) was insufficient to empower them to speak God's word without God having given it to them. Office isn't enough, even if God himself calls the individual.

> For although a man may have many revelations, and
> have power to do many mighty works, yet if he boasts
> in his own strength, and sets at naught the counsels of
> God, and follows after the dictates of his own will and
> carnal desires, he must fall and incur the vengeance of

[13] D&C 50:17-18; see also D&C 20:45
[14] TPJS, p. 112
[15] D&C 42:14
[16] D&C 60:7

27

a just God upon him. (D&C 3:4)

Many personalities in the scriptures, including Judas Iscariot, King Saul, King David, and several Old Testament prophets, had at least seasons where their rebellion led to a dearth in the word of God— sometimes permanently. The truthfulness of messengers is not permanent; their status as a nexus between heaven and earth can be transitory. It is subject to their own status with God and God's ever-changing will.

In Noah's priests we see an example of how false priests, not having a dispensation of God's word, must necessary fill their sermons with misapplied scriptures they do not understand. Samuel the Lamanite tells us that false prophets fill their sermons with praise for people, since they have not received God's word which is always to repent. Though they are sometimes helpful in expounding scripture, platitudes, stories, or personal interpretations are not God's word and are powerless to save in and of themselves.

Let's take a look a the rest of D&C 1, the Lord's preamble to the Doctrine and Covenants:

> And the voice of warning shall be unto all people, by the mouths of my disciples, whom I have chosen in these last days. And they shall go forth and none shall stay them, for *I the Lord have commanded them.* Behold, *this is mine authority, and the authority of my servants,* and my preface unto the book of my commandments, which I have given them to publish unto you, O inhabitants of the earth. (D&C 1:4-6)

The Lord's command *is* the Lord's authority, and the Lord's command is the authority of his servants. Without the Lord's command, his servants have no authority. Without the Lord's command, he has no servants. When one ceases to receive commands from the Lord, one ceases to be the Lord's servant.

Receipt of the continually flowing word of God is essential to increasing faith in the world, as the Lord continues:

> And also gave commandments to others, that they should proclaim these things unto the world; and all this that it might be fulfilled, which was written by the prophets—The weak things of the world shall come forth and break down the mighty and strong ones, that man should not counsel his fellow man, neither trust in the arm of flesh—But that every man might speak in the name of God the Lord, even the Savior of the world; That faith also might increase in the earth; That mine everlasting covenant might be established; (D&C 1:18-22)

The phrase "arm of the flesh" as used in the scriptures refers to the supposed authority, wisdom, or power of men who speak their own words and act in the absence of or in opposition to God's commands. Contrary to implying that a set of men possess God's power independent of his dictations to them,[17] this section condemns those who suppose God has given his power to men

---

[17]This is the devilish doctrine Nephi warned about when he said "they deny the power of God, the Holy One of Israel; and they say unto the people: Hearken unto us, and hear ye our precept; for behold there is no God today, for the Lord and the Redeemer

and that there is any wisdom in hearkening to men whose words do not come from God and who replace God's commandments with their own.

Without faith, no man can please God. Without the word, no man can have faith. This is taught plainly by Joseph Smith in the "Lectures on Faith."[18]

Note how God's word is necessary that his "everlasting covenant might be established." Joseph taught that "[God] set the ordinances to be the same forever and ever, and set Adam to watch over them, to reveal them from heaven to man, or to send angels to reveal them."[19] Thus we see that, in order to be valid, ordinances must be dictated from the throne of God, through his angels, to man. God does not acknowledge ordinances created or modified by man for "I, the Lord, am bound when ye do what I say; but when ye do not what I say, ye have no promise."[20] And again, "I command and men obey not; I revoke and they receive not the blessing."[21]

John the apostle taught that the power of God is found in his word and only in his word. Jesus, he taught, is the one and only mediator—the only being between us and our Father in heaven. "Jesus saith unto him, I am the way, the truth, and the life: no man cometh unto the Father, but by me."[22] Nephi provided a second

---

hath done his work, and he hath given his power unto men;" (2 Nephi 28:5)

[18] See the chapter "Faith on the Word" in this book.
[19] TPJS, p. 168
[20] D&C 82:10
[21] D&C 58:32
[22] John 14:6

witness that he does not delegate this position to any other.[23]

The Lord, in several cases, gives a commandment and then says, "whatsoever is more or less than this, cometh of evil."[24] Because "truth is knowledge of things as they are, and as they were, and as they are to come," and because God is "the Spirit of truth," or the source of all truth available to us, "whatsoever is more or less than this is the spirit of that wicked one who was a liar from the beginning."[25] The words which God utters and are delivered to us are the rock. Words uttered by man are not the rock, but sand. They did not originate from the source of all truth. God will not own them, and in them is no power. The word of God can only lead to life, and the commandments of men can only lead to death. Therefore,

> ...whoso among you shall do more or less than these are not built upon my rock, but are built upon a sandy foundation; and when the rain descends, and the floods come, and the winds blow, and beat upon them, they shall fall, and the gates of hell are ready open to receive them. (3 Nephi 18:13)

Let us build upon the rock.

---

[23]O then, my beloved brethren, come unto the Lord, the Holy One. Remember that his paths are righteous. Behold, the way for man is narrow, but it lieth in a straight course before him, and the keeper of the gate is the Holy One of Israel; and *he employeth no servant there*; and there is none other way save it be by the gate; for he cannot be deceived, for the Lord God is his name. (2 Nephi 9:41)

[24]D&C 98:7, D&C 124:120, 3 Nephi 18:13, 3 Nephi 11:40

[25]D&C 93:24-26

Power in the Priesthood

"...where the word of a king is, there is power."

—Ecclesiastes 8:4

Priesthood is nothing more and nothing less than the power of God. When God delegates this power to a person or a group of people, it is through his word. John the Baptist was sent from God with a dispensation of God's word to Joseph Smith and Oliver Cowdery. Joseph and Oliver received God's word, which empowered them to do certain things. Peter, James, and John were sent from God's presence to Joseph Smith and Oliver Cowdery. They transmitted to Joseph and Oliver God's word empowering them to do certain things. If Joseph or Oliver had assumed that God authorized them to do these certain things without God actually saying so, their administration would have been in vain. Likewise, if they had assumed more than what God's word had authorized them, or if they had modified the instructions they received, those actions done would have been without power. This is because God does not give his power autonomously to men. He instructs them in true principles, which are then available for the discharge of anyone who obtains those instructions in their correct form. He also, from time to time, authorizes specific actions to specific people. Sometimes that authorization expands beyond the person who receives it, as when he gave the Aaronic priesthood to Aaron and his seed after him.

Every scriptural example accords with this fact. In each case of an exercise of God's power, we find a man who received God's word empowering him to do so.

It is not enough to impersonate the actions of those to whom God has actually spoken. Consider what happened when the sons of Sceva attempted to work the miracles they had observed at the hands of Jesus' disciples. Their actions were emulations of the disciples, yet they had not received God's word to empower their works, as had the disciples:

> Then certain of the vagabond Jews, exorcists, took upon them to call over them which had evil spirits the name of the Lord Jesus, saying, We adjure you by Jesus whom Paul preacheth. And there were seven sons of one Sceva, a Jew, and chief of the priests, which did so. And the evil spirit answered and said, Jesus I know, and Paul I know; but who are ye? And the man in whom the evil spirit was leaped on them, and overcame them, and prevailed against them, so that they fled out of that house naked and wounded. (Acts 19:13-16)

Though the sons of Sceva invoked the name of Jesus, Jesus had not ordained a law whereby the devils would be subject to them. They exercised the same form as those who had a dispensation of God's word, but they had no power. Exercising forms without power is a sin every man should watch for. Joseph once observed Elders repeatedly administering to the sick without healing them. He remarked, "Let the Elders either obtain the power of God to heal the sick, or let them cease to administer the form without the power."[1] In this light, we read the following scripture differently:

> Seek not to declare my word, but first seek to obtain my word, and then shall your tongue be loosed; then, if you desire, you shall have my Spirit and my word, yea, the power of God unto the convincing of men. (D&C 11:21)

When you seek to obtain God's word and then receive it, you will obtained the power of God.

As the sons of Sceva learned, no miracles can be performed save God performs them.

> ...by his word the heaven and the earth should be; and by the power of his word man was created of the dust of the earth; and by the power of his word have miracles been wrought? (Mormon 9:17)

It is impossible for a man to be an instrument in the hands of God without revelation to that end. The object of communication is the word of God. That's why we find so many declarations of the power of God being by his word. Mormon taught:

---

[1] "Autobiography of Joseph Bates Noble," see also "Autobiography of P.P. Pratt."

And he knoweth their prayers, that they were in behalf of their brethren. And he knoweth their faith, for *in his name* could they remove mountains; and *in his name* could they cause the earth to shake; and *by the power of his word* did they cause prisons to tumble to the earth; yea, even the fiery furnace could not harm them, neither wild beasts nor poisonous serpents, *because of the power of his word.* (Mormon 8:24)

Nephi exclaimed that it is

...*by the power of his almighty word* he can cause the earth that it shall pass away; yea, and ye know that *by his word* he can cause the rough places to be made smooth, and smooth places shall be broken up. O, then, why is it, that ye can be so hard in your hearts? (1 Nephi 17:46)

Nephi doesn't explain the priesthood as some institution divorced from God. In fact, he does quite the opposite. He describes the priesthood as being the manifestation of the living link between the throne of heaven and a man on the footstool of earth, a link consisting of the word of God. He warned us not to think that God had given his authority to man and removed himself from the process of exercising his power:

And they deny the power of God, the Holy One of Israel; and they say unto the people: Hearken unto us, and hear ye our precept; for behold there is no God today, for the Lord and the Redeemer hath done his work, and he hath given his power unto men; (2 Nephi 28:5)

If Nephi's witness is still insufficient, we have God's witness that it is "...at my command the heavens are opened and are shut; and at my word the earth shall shake; and at my command the inhabitants thereof shall pass away, even so as by fire."[2]

Priesthood is not a permission slip that entitles the holder to do what he will with minimal or no interaction from God. We should take Nephi as an authority. We would be hard pressed to find any who manifested as much priesthood power as Nephi. His brother, who had seen Christ and wasn't a whit behind Nephi, echoed the same doctrine. Jacob says God created man and the earth "by the power of his word."

> Wherefore, if God being able to speak and the world was, and to speak and man was created, O then, why not able to command the earth, or the workmanship of his hands upon the face of it, according to his will and pleasure? (Jacob 4:9)

This is why Nephi pegged any of his priestly works as being predicated upon God's command:

> ...If God had commanded me to do all things I could do them. If he should command me that I should say unto this water, be thou earth, it should be earth; and if I should say it, it would be done. (1 Nephi 17:50)

---

[2] Ether 4:9

Brigham Young taught similarly that priesthood power is to be found only in the dictations of God to men:

> All the works of mankind amount to but little, unless they are performed in the name of the Lord and under the direction of his Spirit. Let every man seek to learn the things of God by the revelations of Jesus Christ to himself. (JD 10:1)

Not even Jesus Christ was immune to this law. He was only empowered to do what the Father told him to do.

> Believest thou not that I am in the Father, and the Father in me? the words that I speak unto you I speak not of myself: but the Father that dwelleth in me, he doeth the works. (John 14:10)

Teaching about the Savior, Brigham Young said,

> He did nothing of himself. He wrought miracles and performed a good work on the earth; but of himself he did nothing. He said, 'As I have seen my Father do, so do I.' 'I came not to do my will, but the will of him that sent me.' We must come to the conclusion that the Son of God did not suggest, dictate, act, or produce any manifestation of his power, of his glory, or of his errand upon the earth, only as it came from the mind and will of his Father. (Brigham Young, JD 6:96)

and again,

He has died to redeem it, and he is the lawful heir pertaining to this earth. Jesus will continue to reign with his Father, and is dictated by his Father in all his acts and ruling and governing in the building up and overthrow of nations, to make the wrath of man praise him, until he brings all into subjection to his will and government. And when he has subdued all his enemies, destroyed death and him that hath the power of death, and perfected his work, he will deliver up the kingdom spotless to his Father. (Brigham Young, JD 7:144)

Jesus could only do those things contained in Heavenly Father's word to him. If Jesus Christ is subject to this law, are any of us exempt?

And thus we see that no amount of priesthood ordination can ever give a man power to use God's power in a way other than which God has ordained. So priesthood is not a dispensation of power to man, but rather the result when man obtains and yields to the word of God. To illustrate the point, consider Mormon's soliloquy about the insubordination of men found in Helaman 12:

O how great is the nothingness of the children of men; yea, even they are less than the dust of the earth. For behold, the dust of the earth moveth hither and thither, to the dividing asunder, at the command of our great and everlasting God. Yea, behold at his voice do the hills and the mountains tremble and quake. And by the power of his voice they are broken up, and become smooth, yea, even like unto a valley. Yea, by the power of his voice doth the whole earth shake; Yea, by the power of his voice, do the foundations rock, even to the very center. Yea, and if he say unto the earth—Move—it is moved. Yea, if he say unto the earth—Thou shalt go back, that it lengthen out the day for many hours—it is done; And thus, according to his word the earth goeth back, and it appeareth unto man that the sun standeth still; yea, and behold, this is so; for surely it is the earth that moveth and not the sun. And behold, also, if he say unto the waters of the great deep—Be thou dried up—it is done. Behold, if he say unto this mountain—Be thou raised up, and come over and fall upon that city, that it be buried up—behold it is done. And behold, if a man hide up a treasure in the earth, and the Lord shall say—Let it be accursed, because of the iniquity of him who hath hid it up—behold, it shall be accursed. And if the Lord shall say—Be thou accursed, that no man shall find thee from this time henceforth and forever—behold, no man getteth it henceforth and forever. (Helaman 12:7-19)

His words make it abundantly clear that all of God's creations save one—us—readily respond to his word. As opposed to the rest of creation, men have generally opted to use their agency against God's instructions. However, as we seek for God's word and yield to it, we will find ourselves necessitating the exercise of God's power to fulfill God's command. This is not the fulfillment of our vain desires, but, as Moses was given power over water that he might enable God's people to cross the sea, we will find ourselves doing God's work for God's purposes.

God's word is *the* mechanism of power in our universe. There is not a single true principle, law, movement, advancement, or joy in this world that did not come into being as a result of God's word. This is as true in spiritual settings as temporal. All temporal laws came into being by God's word. Through the medium of the spirit of God, which is in all things and through all things, temporal actions occur. When I hit a hammer with a nail, it is the spirit of God working with the temporal matter of the artifacts in play that causes the nail to drive into the wood. When I take a match to dry paper, it is the spirit of God acting through the medium of the match, the chemicals in the air, and the matter of the paper to ignite. Whenever you do anything in this world, you can correctly see it as matter obeying God's word as it has been given to it. Since the power of God is what actuates everything we do,[3] it turns out that man cannot act at all without using some power God has given him. Acts as simple as taking a breath would be impossible without our bodies being sustained by the laws he has ordained by his word. As I type this page, I do so by taking advantage of the power he has given me to think, to breathe, and to move. We are quick to overlook that, in this non-trivial sense, everyone has some amount of priesthood: that portion of the power of God given to every man. This dispensation of power is

---

[3] "I say unto you that if ye should serve him who has created you from the beginning, and is preserving you from day to day, by lending you breath, that ye may live and move and do according to your own will, and even supporting you from one moment to another—I say, if ye should serve him with all your whole souls yet ye would be unprofitable servants." (Mosiah 2:21)

bound by certain laws: I cannot jump 400 feet. I cannot avoid the effects of gravity. I cannot speak a foreign language I do not know.

However, our descriptions of priesthood generally focus on power given to God that breaks the rules that apply to the power he gives generally. An angel can jump 400 feet and defy gravity. God can, through the Holy Ghost, enable a man to speak a language he has not learned. Actions such as raising the dead, moving mountains, spontaneously communicating in an unknown tongue, closing the mouths of lions, healing the sick, and so on, like the rest, are controlled by God's word. He has not put these actions into man's power. Unlike the other things discussed, these actions were not instructed through his word at the creation to yield to man. They require a new dispensation of his word in order to take place. These permissions are no less bound by his law than the general powers granted to man. However, the law applies to an individual, and not to the general population. Moses could divide the waters. Aaron could not. Joseph received revelations from the heavens. Oliver did not.

Priesthood is nothing more and nothing less than the transmittance of God's word from his throne to an individual, empowering them to use that dispensed word to unlock normally locked experiences. "By the power of his word miracles [are] wrought," Mormon says. It is "by his word" that he commanded that "the heaven and the earth should be" and "by the power of his word man was created of the dust of the earth."[4] And so we see the brother of Jared experiencing the miraculous because of what God had said to him:

---

[4]Mormon 9:17

And behold, we have seen in this record that one of these was the brother of Jared; for so great was his faith in God, that when God put forth his finger he could not hide it from the sight of the brother of Jared, because of his word which he had spoken unto him, which word he had obtained by faith. (Ether 12:20)

We see the same with every man who received God's power. Enoch was given God's word which enabled him to conduct many of the actions that are locked by default from mankind:

And so great was the faith of Enoch that he led the people of God, and their enemies came to battle against them; and he spake the word of the Lord, and the earth trembled, and the mountains fled, even according to his command; and the rivers of water were turned out of their course; and the roar of the lions was heard out of the wilderness; and all nations feared greatly, so powerful was the word of Enoch, and *so great was the power of the language which God had given him.* (Moses 7:13)

The language of God—the words of God—is the authority of God. As described above, the individual receiving it acts on the same principle as the engineer works on the effect of gravity or the metallurgist works on the laws of thermodynamics.

It is of worth to note that there are uncommon experiences that are seen as supernatural that ought not be uncommon. In addition to ordaining his power to every man to do things like write or speak or breathe, God has also ordained that several actions—what we would call miracles—might be done without any further communication on his part. He has said this of those who believe:

> And these signs shall follow them that believe—In my name they shall do many wonderful works; In my name they shall cast out devils; In my name they shall heal the sick; In my name they shall open the eyes of the blind, and unstop the ears of the deaf; And the tongue of the dumb shall speak; And if any man shall administer poison unto them it shall not hurt them; And the poison of a serpent shall not have power to harm them. (D&C 84:65-72)

Although the Lord does not say that every time they attempt these things they will be done (in fact he explicitly mentions at least one time when the sick will not be healed—when they are ordained to death), he does not condition any of these occasional miracles on priesthood. His word, in this case, has already been ordained to man, just as he doesn't need to reveal to a skydiver that he will fall out of the sky for him to be subject to gravity.

Since priesthood power is only to be found in the revelation of God's word, the Holy Ghost has a critical role in its exercise. First, the spirit of God that is in all things and through all things is the not only the source of the command that preceeds the action, but it is also the means by which the action takes effect. Christ demonstrated this principle when he healed those he could not see and who could not hear him simply by speaking.[5] And thus

---

[5] "The centurion answered and said, Lord, I am not worthy that thou shouldest come under my roof: but speak the word only, and

we see that God's word is effective at any distance.

Beyond the exercise of the priesthood, the Holy Ghost has a critical role even in the conferral of priesthood. We are told in several locations in scripture that priesthood was ordained "by the power of the Holy Ghost, which was in" those who conferred it.[6]

In conclusion, we must admit that Joseph knew what he was doing when he said: "The Savior has the words of eternal life. Nothing else can profit us....A man can do nothing for himself unless God direct him in the right way; and the Priesthood is for that purpose."[7]

---

my servant shall be healed." (Matthew 8:8)

[6]Moroni 3:4, D&C 20:60, D&C 90:11

[7]TPJS, p. 364

God's Name in Vain

"Jehovah will cut off from Israel head and tail, palm
top and reed, in a single day; the elders or notables are
the head, the prophets who teach falsehoods, the tail.
The leaders of these people have misled them, and
those who are led are confused."

–Isaiah 9:14–16

Ancient Israel was plagued by false prophets and false elders.
Heeding their lying words is what led to the loss of God's blessings
among them. Just as heeding the word of God leads to him,
heeding the words of men and devils leads away from God. Israel
never learned how to differentiate between the word of God and
the word of men. Surely, there is a difference. The words of God
emanate from God's throne and carry with them power. The
words of men are hollow. They not only do not lead a man to
eternal life, but they often distract him with performances that
keep him from seeking and keeping God's word.

But woe unto you, scribes and Pharisees, hypocrites!

47

> for ye shut up the kingdom of heaven against men: for
> ye neither go in yourselves, neither suffer ye them that
> are entering to go in. (Matthew 23:13)

The devil tempts men as far as he can. When he can't get men
to commit grave sins, he tries to convince them to spend their
time in benign pursuits to keep them away from those things that
will save them. Jesus taught plainly and frequently against the
commandments of men, noting that they almost always prevent
the observer from approaching God.

> Then came together unto him the Pharisees, and cer-
> tain of the scribes, which came from Jerusalem. And
> when they saw some of his disciples eat bread with de-
> filed, that is to say, with unwashen, hands, they found
> fault. For the Pharisees, and all the Jews, except they
> wash their hands oft, eat not, holding the tradition
> of the elders. And when they come from the market,
> except they wash, they eat not. And many other things
> there be, which they have received to hold, as the wash-
> ing of cups, and pots, brasen vessels, and of tables.
> Then the Pharisees and scribes asked him, Why walk
> not thy disciples according to the tradition of the el-
> ders, but eat bread with unwashen hands? He answered
> and said unto them, Well hath Esaias prophesied of
> you hypocrites, as it is written, This people honoureth
> me with their lips, but their heart is far from me. How-
> beit in vain do they worship me, teaching for doctrines
> the commandments of men. For laying aside the com-
> mandment of God, ye hold the tradition of men, as

48

the washing of pots and cups: and many other such like things ye do. And he said unto them, <u>Full well ye reject the commandment of God, that ye may keep your own tradition</u>. For Moses said, Honour thy father and thy mother; and, Whoso curseth father or mother, let him die the death: But ye say, If a man shall say to his father or mother, It is Corban, that is to say, a gift, by whatsoever thou mightest be profited by me; he shall be free. And ye suffer him no more to do ought for his father or his mother; <u>Making the word of God of none effect through your tradition, which ye have delivered</u>: and many such like things do ye. (Mark 7:1-13)

Those who honor the commandments of men honor God with their lips, but their hearts are far from him. <u>Those who are most righteous according to the law of men are almost always the furthest from God</u>. Exceptions, of course, exist, such as Paul when he was known as Saul, who was:

Circumcised the eighth day, of the stock of Israel, of the tribe of Benjamin, an Hebrew of the Hebrews; as touching the law, a Pharisee; Concerning zeal, persecuting the church; touching the righteousness which is in the law, blameless.

By and large, however, these men are forced to set aside God's commandments in order to obey the contradictory commandments of men.

49

The commandments of men come from false messengers—those who pretend to be sent from God but have not been given his words to speak, "For he whom God hath sent speaketh the words of God:"[1] For example, the pretended prophets in Jeremiah's day prophesied against the truth—that God was angry with the people—and instead preached what they wanted to hear. "Therefore hearken not unto the words of the prophets that speak unto you, saying, Ye shall not serve the king of Babylon: for they prophesy a lie unto you."[2] This is a hallmark of the fodder of false prophets. They preach that all is well in Zion.[3] If all were well in Zion, the Lord would frequently appear to all citizens of Zion. It's a self-evident situation. Instead, false prophets must announce that all is well in Zion in order to assuage the fears of the people, who are surrounded by evidences of God's displeasure. God's words are almost always a call to repentance, and his true messengers deliver these words, which are hardly ever well-received and never pleasing to the world. Samuel the Lamanite preached how we have a tendency to reject true prophets' hard messages.

> Behold ye are worse than they; for as the Lord liveth,
> if a prophet come among you and declareth unto you
> the word of the Lord, which testifieth of your sins and
> iniquities, ye are angry with him, and cast him out and
> seek all manner of ways to destroy him; yea, you will

---

[1] John 3:34
[2] Jeremiah 27:14
[3] "And others will he pacify, and lull them away into carnal security, that they will say: All is well in Zion; yea, Zion prospereth, all is well—and thus the devil cheateth their souls, and leadeth them away carefully down to hell." (2 Nephi 28:21)

say that he is a false prophet, and that he is a sinner, and of the devil, because he testifieth that your deeds are evil. But behold, if a man shall come among you and shall say: Do this, and there is no iniquity; do that and ye shall not suffer; yea, he will say: Walk after the pride of your own hearts; yea, walk after the pride of your eyes, and do whatsoever your heart desireth—and if a man shall come among you and say this, ye will receive him, and say that he is a prophet. Yea, ye will lift him up, and ye will give unto him of your substance; ye will give unto him of your gold, and of your silver, and ye will clothe him with costly apparel; and because he speaketh flattering words unto you, and he saith that all is well, then ye will not find fault with him. (Helaman 13:26-28)

According to Samuel the Lamanite, we not only are prone to reject true prophets, but we throw treasure and glory to false prophets who satisfy our vanity and sinful desires by telling us how great we are.

False prophets have not been given the true word of God, so they must preach something else to the people. Many times, their substituted message is whatever the people want to hear. Vain men want to dictate to God what message he has for them. However, it doesn't work that way, as evidenced with Balak, who wanted Balaam, a prophet, to prophesy good things for his people against God's will. "And Balaam said unto Balak, Lo, I am come unto thee: have I now any power at all to say any thing? the word that God putteth in my mouth, that shall I speak."[4] Other times, instead of preaching the powerful word of God, which can be pleasing but is hardly entertaining, they preach entertaining fables and stories. Nephi quoted Isaiah's account of how the false prophets were channeling familiar spirits instead of preaching God's word.

> Behold, I and the children whom the Lord hath given me are for signs and for wonders in Israel from the Lord of Hosts, which dwelleth in Mount Zion. And when they shall say unto you: Seek unto them that have familiar spirits, and unto wizards that peep and mutter—should not a people seek unto their God for the living to hear from the dead? To the law and to the testimony; and if they speak not according to this word, it is because there is no light in them. (2 Nephi 18:18-20)

False prophets will resort to any text to avoid speaking of the law and the testimony—God's word through scripture and personal experience—because they do not know the scriptures and have not had personal experiences with God.

It is a mistake to assume that all false prophets are wicked liars. Many are, in fact, well-intentioned. These teach words which they assume are God's through accepting the false traditions of their fathers without establishing a relationship with God themselves in order to expose them as such. These are just as detrimental to the people as those who are liars, despite the fact that their

---

[4]Numbers 22:38

motives are good, because the end result for the people is the same—damnation. Mormon had strong words for such:

> O ye wicked and perverse and stiffnecked people, why have ye built up churches unto yourselves to get gain? Why have ye transfigured the holy word of God, that ye might bring damnation upon your souls? Behold, look ye unto the revelations of God; for behold, the time cometh at that day when all these things must be fulfilled. (Mormon 8:33)

The Lord himself said this about those who ignore God's word:

> And he that will contend against the word of the Lord, let him be accursed; and he that shall deny these things, let him be accursed; for unto them will I show no greater things, saith Jesus Christ; for I am he who speaketh.(Ether 4:8)

You cannot be saved in ignorance.[5] Without the living water of God's word, the vine withers and dies. Brigham Young taught that the only way to counteract false traditions is to get revelation about it and assume ourselves fools before God:

> But we should all live so that the Spirit of revelation could dictate and write on the heart and tell us what we should do instead of the traditions of our parents and teachers. But to do this we must become like little

---

[5] "It is impossible for a man to be saved in ignorance." (D&C 131:6)

children; and Jesus says if we do not we cannot enter
the kingdom of heaven. (Brigham Young, JD 14:161)

Such an approach is sure to earn the wrath of the masses, who
would rather keep their hope in the false traditions of their fathers.

<u>Taking a position of devotion to God's word is always an
unpopular move</u>. Through the scriptures we encounter individuals
who were always alone: hiding in caves, living in the wilderness,
or hunted from place to place because they refused to hearken to
the commandments of men. They were cast into fiery furnaces,
thrown into dens of lions, kicked out of the synagogue, and stoned
for the sake of holding to God's word despite contrary popular
opinion.

Joseph, who himself died because he refused to recant God's
unpopular word, said:

I...spoke to the people, showing them that to get salvation we must not only do some things, but everything
which God has commanded. Men may preach and
practice everything except those things which God
commands us to do, and will be damned at last. We
may tithe mint and rue, and all manner of herbs, and
still not obey the commandments of God. The object
with me is to obey and teach others to obey God in
just what He tells us to do. It mattereth not whether
the principle is popular or unpopular, I will always
maintain a true principle, even if I stand alone in it.
(TPJS p. 332, DHC 6:223)

Yet, despite the guarantee of rejection from the world, believers are commanded to fear God more than men: "For, behold, you should not have feared man more than God. Although men set at naught the counsels of God, and despise his words."[6]

Preaching the commandments of men, we learn from Joseph, happens as much in modern times as it did anciently, and is just as much of an abomination in God's sight as it ever was.

> I was answered that I must join none of them, for they were all wrong; and the Personage who addressed me said that all their creeds were an abomination in his sight; that those professors were all corrupt; that: "they draw near to me with their lips, but their hearts are far from me, they teach for doctrines the commandments of men, having a form of godliness, but they deny the power thereof." (JS-H 1:19)

God said that this condition of apostasy—as all apostasy—occurred because men took his word lightly, hearkening unto their own thoughts and opinions instead of seeking to live by what God had told them, which he has commanded us to obey word for word: "For you shall live by every word that proceedeth forth from the mouth of God."[7] He gave a witness that the time Joseph Smith was raised up would be a time when men would esteem his words as naught:

> And in a day when the children of men shall esteem
> my words as naught and take many of them from the

---

[6]D&C 3:7
[7]D&C 84:44

book which thou shalt write, behold, I will raise up another like unto thee; and they shall be had again among the children of men—among as many as shall believe. (Moses 1:41)

Ignoring God's word results in a lack of power, because God's word is the vehicle for his power. Without God's word, there is none of God's power.

And if any man shall seek to build up himself, and seeketh not my counsel, he shall have no power, and his folly shall be made manifest. Keep yourselves from evil to take the name of the Lord in vain, for I am the Lord your God, even the God of your fathers, the God of Abraham and of Isaac and of Jacob. (D&C 136:19,21)

Note that God considers the claim of his power when his word is not present to be taking his name in vain. Vanity means something without effect. When we invent words that we claim came from God, they are powerless. "Thou shalt not take the name of the Lord thy God in vain: for the Lord will not hold him guiltless that taketh his name in vain."[8] Jesus said that everything in this world that is not by his name shall be thrown down and destroyed. This includes all things that are established by using his name in vain.

And everything that is in the world, whether it be or- dained of men, by thrones, or principalities, or powers,

---

[8]Deuteronomy 5:11

or things of name, whatsoever they may be, that are
not by me or by my word, saith the Lord, shall be
thrown down, and shall not remain after men are dead,
neither in nor after the resurrection, saith the Lord
your God. For whatsoever things remain are by me;
and whatsoever things are not by me shall be shaken
and destroyed. (D&C 132:13-14)

Though the details are outside the scope of this book, it is worth
noting that thrones, principalities, and powers refer to classes of
angels. Do you realize what God is saying here? <u>Not even angels
are authorized to speak outside of what God tells them</u>. If they do,
it is of naught. <u>If angels have the capacity to speak words other
than God's words, how much more so men</u>? As God said, "Cursed
is he that putteth his trust in man, or maketh flesh his arm, or
shall hearken unto the precepts of men, save their precepts shall
be given by the power of the Holy Ghost."[9]

God said that acting with the forms but without the power is a
sin that has occurred in our day: In our search for the word of God,
we have to be constantly on the lookout for the commandments
of men. The Lord taught us to do so by asking God that we might
know the source of what we hear.

But ye are commanded in all things to ask of God, who
giveth liberally; and that which the Spirit testifies unto
you even so I would that ye should do in all holiness
of heart, walking uprightly before me, considering the
end of your salvation, doing all things with prayer and

---

[9] 2 Nephi 28:31

thanksgiving, that ye may not be seduced by evil spirits, or doctrines of devils, or the commandments of men; for some are of men, and others of devils. (D&C 46:7)

And again,

Behold, I am Alpha and Omega, even Jesus Christ. Wherefore, let all men beware how they take my name in their lips— For behold, verily I say, that many there be who are under this condemnation, who use the name of the Lord, and use it in vain, having not authority. Wherefore, let the church repent of their sins, and I, the Lord, will own them; otherwise they shall be cut off. (D&C 63:60-63)

Yet, we are promised again and again that if we keep his word, his words will abide in us, and we will be given power to do what he says. "If ye abide in me, and my words abide in you, ye shall ask what ye will, and it shall be done unto you."[10] Note that the individual's oneness with God ("abide in me") and the presence of God's word to that individual are prerequisites to "asking what ye will" and having it done, which necessarily limits "what ye will" by what is God's will, which is always manifest by his word. We see this explicitly in Moroni 7:33: "And Christ hath said: If ye will have faith in me ye shall have power to do whatsoever thing is expedient in me."

---

[10]John 15:7

Anxiously Engaged

"Verily I say, men should be anxiously engaged in a
good cause, and do many things of their own free will,
and bring to pass much righteousness;"

–D&C 58:27

The Lord said, "For behold, it is not meet that I should command in all things; for he that is compelled in all things, the same is a slothful and not a wise servant; wherefore he receiveth no reward."[1] We are told that we are independent agents and we ought to be "anxiously engaged in a good cause" of our "own free will" to "bring to pass much righteousness." That notion, in and of itself, is correct. However, far too many seek to implement it by leaving God out of the equation. They interpret the Lord's instruction to mean that we ought to have two parallel channels of action: One channel where we consistently await any impromptu revelation to do good, and one channel where we go about doing what we think we ought to do to bring to pass much righteousness.

---

[1] D&C 58:27

59

This is not the intent of the scripture, and following this path will always lead to far fewer interactions with heaven than God would have us receive.

God is not telling us that we ought not to seek to be dictated in all things. Those who do not desire more of God's direction in life are those of whom Nephi spoke when he said, "Wo be unto him that shall say: We have received the word of God, and we need no more of the word of God, for we have enough!"[2] What he is saying is that we should not rely on his impromptu revelations to guide us in all things. Those who do so are slothful. Rather, life is not a passive existence, and we ought to seek out God and be proactive in seeking his guidance. Nephi taught:

> But behold, I say unto you that ye must pray always, and not faint; that ye must not perform any thing unto the Lord save in the first place ye shall pray unto the Father in the name of Christ, that he will consecrate thy performance unto thee, that thy performance may be for the welfare of thy soul. (2 Nephi 32:9)

This is hardly a message to go about doing things without involving God. We ought to be observing the world, seeking to do good, and asking him all sorts of questions to know the best way to go about it. The Lord told us that "all things must be done in the name of Christ, whatsoever you do in the Spirit;"[3] Moroni said, "see that ye do all things in worthiness, and do it in the name of Jesus Christ, the Son of the living God."[4] How can we do

---

[2] 2 Nephi 28:29
[3] D&C 46:31
[4] Mormon 9:29

something in the name of Christ if Christ has not told us to do it? Asking him, it turns out, is a key to receiving God's word for us: Personal revelation to dictate us in all things.

The holy men of the scriptures are great examples of this principle. They sought revelation on what to do, and they followed it in God's power, having received his word. Joseph Smith said,

> Abraham was guided in all his family affairs by the Lord; was conversed with by angels, and by the Lord; was told where to go, and when to stop; and prospered exceedingly in all that he put his hand unto; it was because he and his family obeyed the counsel of the Lord. (TPJS, pp. 252-253)

If father Abraham was guided in all his affairs, including the temporal ones, ought we not to seek the same? Was Jesus Christ himself not commanded in all things? He said,

> The Son can do nothing of himself, but what he seeth the Father do: for what things soever he doeth, these also doeth the Son likewise. For the Father loveth the Son, and sheweth him all things that himself doeth. (John 5:19-20)

Brigham Young frequently preached that we ought to seek revelation from God that we may be dictated in all matters.[5] On one occasion, he taught:

---

[5]Several quotes from him on that topic are available elsewhere in this book.

I will, in the commencement of my remarks, take up a subject upon which much has been said in the pulpit and in the chimney corner. It is regarding the Spirit of the Lord manifesting his will to his children. There is no doubt, if a person lives according to the revelations given to God's people, he may have the Spirit of the Lord to signify to him his will, and to guide and to direct him in the discharge of his duties, in his temporal as well as his spiritual exercises. I am satisfied, however, that in this respect, we live far beneath our privileges. (JD 12:104)

Seeking to be dictated is much more than a passive waiting process. Isaiah wrote "And thine ears shall hear a word behind thee, saying, This is the way, walk ye in it, when ye turn to the right hand, and when ye turn to the left."[6] The promise here is that if you are already moving, God will speak to you and guide your paths. The sons of Mosiah lived this principle when they decided to go serve a mission among the Lamanites. The confirmation from God for their trip did not come until they were already many days into their journey:

And it came to pass that they journeyed many days in the wilderness, and they fasted much and prayed much that the Lord would grant unto them a portion of his Spirit to go with them, and abide with them, that they might be an instrument in the hands of God to bring, if it were possible, their brethren, the Lamanites,

---

[6]Isaiah 30:21

to the knowledge of the truth, to the knowledge of the baseness of the traditions of their fathers, which were not correct. And it came to pass that the Lord did visit them with his Spirit, and said unto them: Be comforted. And they were comforted. And the Lord said unto them also: Go forth among the Lamanites, thy brethren, and establish my word; yet ye shall be patient in long-suffering and afflictions, that ye may show forth good examples unto them in me, and I will make an instrument of thee in my hands unto the salvation of many souls. (Alma 17:9-11)

The best example of what it means is given to us by the Savior. In the premortal councils, he did not wait for the Father to announce a plan. He suggested one that best fit what he understood about the Father's will and character. The Father accepted it, dispensing his word to empower Christ to accomplish it. Obedience is not just agreeing to what God tells us. It means actively searching—with all our faculties—to learn God's will, while seeking his word on it prior to our accomplishing it.

Faith on His Word

"So then faith cometh by hearing, and hearing by the
word of God."

–Romans 10:17

What is faith? It is nothing more and nothing less than receiving God's word and acting in full belief that it is true. This
definition expands our understanding of events as laid out in the
scriptures as examples of faith. Moroni teaches us that "it is by
faith that miracles are wrought," since without a dispensation of
God's word, God's power is not present, and it is God's power
that works miracles.[1] He continues by saying that "it is by faith

---

[1]Even Jesus Christ himself could not work miracles independent of the throne of God. He had to receive the Father's word
to empower him to do all the miracles he did. "He did nothing
of himself. He wrought miracles and performed a good work on
the earth; but of himself he did nothing. He said, 'As I have seen
my Father do, so do I.' 'I came not to do my will, but the will of
him that sent me.' We must come to the conclusion that the Son
of God did not suggest, dictate, act, or produce any manifestation
of his power, of his glory, or of his errand upon the earth, only as

that angels appear and minister unto men," "For behold, they are subject unto him, to minister according to the word of his command, showing themselves unto them of strong faith and a firm mind in every form of godliness."[2] Noah received God's word that a flood was coming. He believed God, and acted on the instructions he received to build the ark.

> By faith Noah, being warned of God of things not seen as yet, moved with fear, prepared an ark to the saving of his house; by the which he condemned the world, and became heir of the righteousness which is by faith. (Hebrews 11:7)

It was by faith that "Isaac blessed Jacob and Esau concerning things to come."[3] He knew of those things to come because God had told him, and he believed God that they would actually happen. The miraculous appearance to the brother of Jared came first by God giving him his word and second by the brother of Jared believing it:

> And behold, we have seen in this record that one of these was the brother of Jared; for so great was his faith in God, that when God put forth his finger he could not hide it from the sight of the brother of Jared, *because of his word which he had spoken unto him,* which word he had obtained by faith. (Ether 12:20)

---

it came from the mind and will of his Father." (Brigham Young, JD 6:96)

[2] Moroni 7:37, Moroni 7:30
[3] Hebrews 11:20

66

Holy men of all times have worked miracles by faith, first obtaining God's word to them authorizing them to do certain things, and second acting in belief that God was true to his word:

> And he knoweth their prayers, that they were in behalf of their brethren. And he knoweth their faith, for in his name could they remove mountains; and in his name could they cause the earth to shake; and by the power of his word did they cause prisons to tumble to the earth; yea, even the fiery furnace could not harm them, neither wild beasts nor poisonous serpents, because of the power of his word. (Mormon 8:24)

Finally, and most important, it is by faith in Christ's name that men are saved and become sons of God.[4] This is because the pathway to salvation consists of God's word (his commandments or instructions), which the voyager must seek and heed in order to obtain divine sonship and redemption from the fall. To sum up: "Faith comes by hearing the word of God, through the testimony of the servants of God; that testimony is always attended by the Spirit of prophecy and revelation."[5]

What isn't faith? You cannot have faith in something that isn't God's word. As an example of this, in Lecture 2 of "Lectures on Faith," Joseph teaches the difference between Abel's sacrifice, which God accepted, and Cain's sacrifice, which he did not. Both Abel and Cain were taught by God how to make sacrifices (see TPJS, p. 58). However, Cain decided to modify the instructions

---

[4] Moroni 7:26
[5] HC, 3:379

he received. Instead of sacrificing an animal, he sacrificed crops. God did not accept this sacrifice which he had not ordained. Cain changed the ordinance, and it was not acceptable to God. "Without faith no man pleaseth God;"[6] Without God's word to you, and your belief in it to heed it, you cannot please God. If any part of that equation is changed, the connection with God is broken. If you do not receive God's word, or if you change what he has told you, or if you don't believe what he has told you, or if you don't do what he told you, you cannot have faith.

It is not possible to have faith in a false principle. You can only obtain a blessing by obeying the law it is predicated upon.[7] Is there no blessing for those who are zealous about what they have been beguiled to think is God's word, but is truly the word of man? They are always given an opportunity to accept the truth as a result of their zealousness for what they believe is God's word. Consider some proofs from the scriptures. We read of Alma Jr., who went about convincing church members to fight against the church. If the angel of repentance visited Alma Jr. as a result of the prayers of Alma Sr. and the congregation, we would expect this sort of thing to occur anytime a righteous parent and their congregation prays for a wayward soul—after all, God is no respecter of persons. Because we don't see that, we should look for another cause. Alma Jr., like Saul of old, was doing all the wrong things for all the right reasons. Saul (later Paul) boasted that he was perfect with respect to the law of Moses:

---

[6]D&C 63:11

[7]"And when we obtain any blessing from God, it is by obedience to that law upon which it is predicated." D&C 130:21

Though I might also have confidence in the flesh. If any other man thinketh that he hath whereof he might trust in the flesh, I more: Circumcised the eighth day, of the stock of Israel, of the tribe of Benjamin, an Hebrew of the Hebrews; as touching the law, a Pharisee; Concerning zeal, persecuting the church; touching the righteousness which is in the law, blameless. (Philippians 3:4-6)

Paul and Alma Jr. were doing the best they could with the light that they had. Still, they could not have faith in false principles. Saul could not have faith in the stoning of Stephen according to the law of Moses, for it was, in that instance, a false principle. Alma Jr. could not have faith in turning his friends away from the gospel of Christ. However, God mercifully recognized their zeal. They were honest men, although wicked. He condescended to provide further light to them, in both cases sending heavenly messengers to provide extra light and truth.

Interestingly, we do not know whether Abel and Cain were taught directly by God how to make sacrifices, or (more likely) if Adam was taught by an angel, and Adam taught Cain and Abel. If this latter arrangement is correct, it gives us an example of how God's revealed word stays in force as long as men follow it. In other words, the sacrifice of Abel was just as recognized as Adam's sacrifice, because he had not changed the ordinance. It was not Cain's lack of authority that invalidated his sacrifice, but his deviation from the revealed ordinance. This is reminiscent of an event that occurs many years later.

God tells Alma,

> Blessed art thou, Alma, and blessed are they who were
> baptized in the waters of Mormon. Thou art blessed
> because of thy exceeding faith in the words alone of
> my servant Abinadi. (Mosiah 26:15)

Do you realize what things Alma did based alone on the words
(the knowledge he received) from Abinadi? These include extensive
teaching, baptizing, and forming a church.

> And also that king Noah and his priests had caused the
> people to commit so many sins and iniquities against
> God; and they also did mourn for the death of Abinadi;
> and also for the departure of Alma and the people that
> went with him, who had formed a church of God
> through the strength and power of God, and faith on
> the words which had been spoken by Abinadi. (Mosiah
> 21:30)

The word of God was revealed to Abinadi and preached to Alma
(once). Then Abinadi was killed. Even though Abinadi was dead,
God's word which had been given to Alma through Abinadi was
just as valid as if Abinadi had been alive. According to God,
Abinadi's words delivered to the priests (including Alma) were
God's words and the source of all of Alma's preaching, teaching,
baptizing, and church formation. It was sufficient and valid. Alma
did not need a new dispensation of God's word in order to preach,
teach, baptize, or even form a church. What God gave him through
Abinadi was enough for all of that. He had faith in God by hearing
God's word through Abinadi and believing it. "Behold, I can
tell you—did not my father Alma believe in the words which

were delivered by the mouth of Abinadi? And was he not a holy prophet? Did he not speak the words of God, and my father Alma believe them?"[8]

Another example of faith on God's word is found in the sons of Helaman, who were miraculously protected from the Lamanite armies. Since a miracle was performed, and since miracles only occur through faith, and since faith is receiving God's word and acting in belief on it, we can search the story for when these boys received God's word. We find the answer in their mothers. The miracle occurred because:

> ...they did obey and observe to perform every word of command with exactness; yea, and even according to their faith it was done unto them; and I did remember the words which they said unto me that their mothers had taught them. (Alma 57:21)

The miracle would not have occurred if the mothers had said whatever they pleased—if they had made up these words. The author would not have cited this as an example of faith unless God's word predicated the event. And so these mothers obtained a promise from God for the protection of their boys, just as King Mosiah had for his sons. Following the commands of Helaman with exactness would not have bought them anything had God not proclaimed this as a precondition for their blessing. The word of God produced faith for the sons of Helaman despite the time and space that separated the young men from the promise that God gave to their mothers.

---

[8]Alma 5:11

Faith is not bound by time nor space. Alma attained power from God to baptize and start a church based on the word of God through Abinadi, who was then dead. Likewise, Abel was able to practice sacrifice through the instructions of his father, who wasn't around when he did it (which we assume since he certainly was not around for Cain's sacrifice, as he would have forestalled it).

Additionally, we see that all men who are saved are saved because they believed the words of prophets, most of whom are dead, who prophesied concerning the coming of the Lord:

> Behold I say unto you, that whosoever has heard the words of the prophets, yea, all the holy prophets who have prophesied concerning the coming of the Lord—I say unto you, that all those who have hearkened unto their words, and believed that the Lord would redeem his people, and have looked forward to that day for a remission of their sins, I say unto you, that these are his seed, or they are the heirs of the kingdom of God. (Mosiah 15:11)

The validity of the word of God preached through those dead prophets has nothing to do at all with their life or death. It has everything to do with whether their words were from God or not. God's words never fail.[9] The conditions of salvation never change. A man today who listens to the principles upon which Abraham

---

[9]God's word never changes and his utterances are always fulfilled. "And behold, I, the Lord, declare unto you, and my words are sure and shall not fail, that they shall obtain it." (D&C 64:31) "And this is the word which he hath given unto the children of men. And for this cause he fulfilleth the words which he hath

was saved will find himself with the salvation of Abraham. And, should he choose to remove from, add to, or transfigure the word of God, he will find himself without the salvation of Abraham.

---

given, and he lieth not, but fulfilleth all his words." (3 Nephi 27:18) "Although, the days will come, that heaven and earth shall pass away; yet my words shall not pass away, but all shall be fulfilled." (JST Matthew 1:35) "For as I, the Lord God, liveth, even so my words cannot return void, for as they go forth out of my mouth they must be fulfilled." (Moses 4:30) "But remember that all my judgments are not given unto men; and as the words have gone forth out of my mouth even so shall they be fulfilled, that the first shall be last, and that the last shall be first in all things whatsoever I have created by the word of my power, which is the power of my Spirit." (D&C 29:30)

A Fullness of His Word

"...all thy words will I justify..."

–Moses 6:34

What the Fullness is

From time to time throughout the history of the earth, men have lived to whom God has given the fullness of the priesthood. One such man was Enoch. To him God said,

> Behold my Spirit is upon you, wherefore all thy words will I justify; and the mountains shall flee before you, and the rivers shall turn from their course; and thou shalt abide in me, and I in you; therefore walk with me. (Moses 6:34)

In God's word to Enoch, we can dispel several common misconceptions about the fullness. First, God does not give his power to men with no strings attached. It is not a delegation of his power. Instead, as we see above, the qualification for this blessing is that his Spirit (his word, his light, his truth) are upon Enoch. Enoch has absorbed the words of God to such a degree that his words are like unto God's. For that reason, God is able to announce that creation will respond to Enoch as it responds to God. As God dwells in Enoch through the dispensation of his word to Enoch's soul, Enoch dwells in God through the same mechanism. Both personages are tied to each other through the word of God, which they both have absorbed into themselves and heeded to the point of it being the sole actuating force of them both.

God gives us another example of the requirement for the recipient to have sought, obtained, and absorbed the word of God into his very being in the person of Nephi, son of Helaman. He tells Nephi, "all things shall be done unto thee according to thy word, for thou shalt not ask that which is contrary to my will."[1] As with Enoch, God indicates that Nephi has obtained and absorbed enough of God's word that his personality and character have come to be like Christ's. Therefore, he will not ask for that which is contrary to the nature and will of God. Even when God gives his word to someone conveying the fullness of the priesthood, there is no blank check of authority transmitted. We see this over and over again with characters to whom God gives a fullness: they still pray and ask God what to do.

> O Lord, thou didst hearken unto my words when I said, Let there be a famine, that the pestilence of the sword might cease; and I know that thou wilt, even at this time, hearken unto my words, for thou saidst that: If this people repent I will spare them. (Helaman 11:14)

---

[1]Helaman 10:5

They are still subject to his will. Not by force, but because they choose to be. Their power is not autonomous. It is always derived from God through his word, and is always subject to his word and his law.

We may wonder how to obtain this blessing. Jesus taught us how. He said that all who consistently seek and heed his word will also attain the character of God and will be given the fullness. "If ye abide in me, and my words abide in you, ye shall ask what ye will, and it shall be done unto you."[2] This pattern is further explained in D&C 84:

> And I now give unto you a commandment to beware concerning yourselves, to give diligent heed to the words of eternal life. For you shall live by every word that proceedeth forth from the mouth of God. For the word of the Lord is truth, and whatsoever is truth is light, and whatsoever is light is Spirit, even the Spirit of Jesus Christ. And the Spirit giveth light to every man that cometh into the world; and the Spirit enlighteneth every man through the world, that hearkeneth to the voice of the Spirit. And every one that hearkeneth to the voice of the Spirit cometh unto God, even the Father. And the Father teacheth him of the covenant which he has renewed and confirmed upon you, which is confirmed upon you for your sakes, and not for your sakes only, but for the sake of the whole world. (D&C 84:43-48)

---

[2] John 15:7

This description invites us to continually seek and heed the word of God, which is the voice of the Spirit, which is light and truth. All those who do this come to Christ and the Father. This is the process by which the fullness is received.

What the Fullness is Not

The fullness is not an object that can be received, wielded according to the desires of the recipient, and passed to whoever the recipient desires. The only way the fullness can be received is through seeking, obtaining, and heeding the words of God until they become a part of you sufficient to change your very nature. No man can force you to attain the character of God. Not even God will force you to do that. Only the individual has the power to create the environment for this heavenly experience to occur. It is not externally governed. It is an internal process that is punctuated by recognition from heaven via a special dispensation of God's word.

Covenants as Dispensations of God's Word

Covenants are nothing more nor less than God giving promises— his word—to men. God's promise to Nephi and to Enoch were covenants with them. We find no one in scripture—not one individual—who exercised the powers God gave to Enoch without them first having the same experience with God that Enoch had.

Joseph said,

You, no doubt, will agree with us, and say, that you

have no right to claim the promises of the inhabitants before the flood; that you cannot found your hopes of salvation upon the obedience of the children of Israel when journeying in the wilderness, nor can you expect that the blessings which the apostles pronounced upon the churches of Christ eighteen hundred years ago, were intended for you. Again, if others' blessings are not your blessings, others' curses are not your curses; you stand then in these last days, as all have stood before you, agents unto yourselves, to be judged according to your works. (TPJS, p. 12)

Because we cannot dictate the words of God, we cannot initiate a covenant. We can, however, respond to God's invitation to live a certain way, and by so doing come to the point where he makes a covenant with us by declaring his word to us.

God restored the priesthood through Joseph Smith. He did so in two ways: first, he restored to Joseph the authority to ordain to the lower and higher priesthoods. These priesthoods authorize the bearer to organize churches, baptize, etc, but they do not automatically bring you back into the presence of God. For this reason, the second more important restoration of the priesthood through Joseph was the restoration of the knowledge of the covenants God has made with his children. Consider that every account we have of the fullness of the priesthood being conferred from God occurs in scriptures restored by (in the case of the Pearl of Great Price and the Bible translation) or delivered through (in the case of the D&C) Joseph Smith. These covenants are exceedingly important. They are what differentiate our church from the greater restoration movement that was pervasive in Joseph's day.

The Campbellite Christianity of 1830 Kirtland sought to restore the New Testament doctrines of faith, repentance, and baptism. When Joseph arrived, he offered something different. Joseph was not restoring the New Testament church—his mission was to restore the covenant of God with Israel, which covenant was not that a certain genealogical lineage had hope for eternal life, but that God would make a covenant of eternal life with all those who obtained and lived by God's word to them. As God said, "I am the Lord thy God; and I give unto you this commandment—that no man shall come unto the Father but by me or by my word, which is my law, saith the Lord."[3] Interestingly, the Campbellites did not believe that the Holy Ghost was an essential element of salvation. However, it is impossible to receive revelation—and thus covenants—by any other means.

Covenants God Restored Through Joseph

Through Joseph's instrumentality, God restored to us a knowledge of the many covenants he has made with the fathers—those saved beings who sought for and obtained promises on our behalf.

With Noah, God covenanted that Zion would come again as soon as men kept his commandments:

> And the bow shall be in the cloud; and I will look upon it, that I may remember the everlasting covenant, which I made unto thy father Enoch; that, when men

---

[3]D&C 132: 12

should keep all my commandments, Zion should again come on the earth, the city of Enoch which I have caught up unto myself. And this is mine everlasting covenant, that when thy posterity shall embrace the truth, and look upward, then shall Zion look downward, and all the heavens shall shake with gladness, and the earth shall tremble with joy; And the general assembly of the church of the firstborn shall come down out of heaven, and possess the earth, and shall have place until the end come. And this is mine everlasting covenant, which I made with thy father Enoch. And the bow shall be in the cloud, and I will establish my covenant unto thee, which I have made between me and thee, for every living creature of all flesh that shall be upon the earth. And God said unto Noah, This is the token of the covenant which I have established between me and thee; for all flesh that shall be upon the earth. (JST Genesis 9:21-25)

To Joseph of Egypt, God promised that he would raise up a righteous branch from his loins and that Moses would deliver that branch both in the former day and (by another figure like Moses) in the latter day:

And Joseph said unto his brethren, I die, and go unto my fathers; and I go down to my grave with joy. The God of my father Jacob be with you, to deliver you out of affliction in the days of your bondage; for the Lord hath visited me, and I have obtained a promise of the

> Lord, that out of the fruit of my loins, the Lord God
> will raise up a righteous branch out of my loins; and
> unto thee, whom my father Jacob hath named Israel,
> a prophet; (not the Messiah who is called Shilo;) and
> this prophet shall deliver my people out of Egypt in
> the days of thy bondage. (JST Gen 50:24)

Through Joseph Smith, we are told of the promise God made
to Melchizedek that would apply equally to all who received a
fullness of the priesthood, showing not only the manner in which
it is received, but the powers conveyed upon receipt:

> And Melchizedek lifted up his voice and blessed Abram.
> Now Melchizedek was a man of faith, who wrought
> righteousness; and when a child he feared God, and
> stopped the mouths of lions, and quenched the vio-
> lence of fire. And thus, having been approved of God,
> he was ordained an high priest after the order of the
> covenant which God made with Enoch, It being after
> the order of the Son of God; which order came, not by
> man, nor the will of man; neither by father nor mother;
> neither by beginning of days nor end of years; but of
> God; And it was delivered unto men by the calling of
> his own voice, according to his own will, unto as many
> as believed on his name. For God having sworn unto
> Enoch and unto his seed with an oath by himself; that
> every one being ordained after this order and calling
> should have power, by faith, to break mountains, to
> divide the seas, to dry up waters, to turn them out of

their course; To put at defiance the armies of nations, to divide the earth, to break every band, to stand in the presence of God; to do all things according to his will, according to his command, subdue principalities and powers; and this by the will of the Son of God which was from before the foundation of the world. And men having this faith, coming up unto this order of God, were translated and taken up into heaven. And now, Melchizedek was a priest of this order; therefore he obtained peace in Salem, and was called the Prince of peace. And his people wrought righteousness, and obtained heaven, and sought for the city of Enoch which God had before taken, separating it from the earth, having reserved it unto the latter days, or the end of the world; And hath said, and sworn with an oath, that the heavens and the earth should come together; and the sons of God should be tried so as by fire. And this Melchizedek, having thus established righteousness, was called the king of heaven by his people, or, in other words, the King of peace. And he lifted up his voice, and he blessed Abram, being the high priest, and the keeper of the storehouse of God; Him whom God had appointed to receive tithes for the poor. Wherefore, Abram paid unto him tithes of all that he had, of all the riches which he possessed, which God had given him more than that which he had need. And it came to pass, that God blessed Abram, and gave unto him riches, and honor, and lands for an everlasting possession; according to the covenant which he had made, and according to the blessing wherewith Melchizedek had blessed him. (JST Gen 14:25-40)

We learn, through Joseph, of the covenant God made with Abraham promising him posterity and priesthood:

For I am the Lord thy God; I dwell in heaven; the earth is my footstool; I stretch my hand over the sea, and it obeys my voice; I cause the wind and the fire to be my chariot; I say to the mountains—Depart hence—and behold, they are taken away by a whirlwind, in an instant, suddenly. My name is Jehovah, and I know the end from the beginning; therefore my hand shall be over thee. And I will make of thee a great nation, and I will bless thee above measure, and make thy name great among all nations, and thou shalt be a blessing unto thy seed after thee, that in their hands they shall bear this ministry and Priesthood unto all nations; And I will bless them through thy name; for as many as receive this Gospel shall be called after thy name, and shall be accounted thy seed, and shall rise up and bless thee, as their father; And I will bless them that bless thee, and curse them that curse thee; and in thee (that is, in thy Priesthood) and in thy seed (that is, thy Priesthood), for I give unto thee a promise that this right shall continue in thee, and in thy seed after thee (that is to say, the literal seed, or the seed of the body) shall all the families of the earth be blessed, even with the blessings of the Gospel, which are the blessings of salvation, even of life eternal. (Abraham 2:8-11)

In the Book of Mormon, translated by Joseph, we find many of God's promises to the seed of Lehi. Truly Joseph was an instrument for restoring God's covenants.

Covenant Validity through Obedience

Our status as a covenant people is a lot more tenuous than we would like to believe. Paul taught plainly that status as children of the covenant God made with Abraham means that we have exercised faith in Jesus: we have obtained the word of Christ and we have lived the word of Christ.

> That the blessing of Abraham might come on the Gentiles through Jesus Christ; that we might receive the promise of the Spirit through faith. For ye are all the children of God by faith in Christ Jesus. For as many of you as have been baptized into Christ have put on Christ. There is neither Jew nor Greek, there is neither bond nor free, there is neither male nor female: for ye are all one in Christ Jesus. And if ye be Christ's, then are ye Abraham's seed, and heirs according to the promise. (Galatians 3:14, 26-29)

Nephi stresses this same teaching: covenant status is available to all who will repent:

> For behold, I say unto you that as many of the Gentiles as will repent are the covenant people of the Lord; and

as many of the Jews as will not repent shall be cast off; for the Lord covenanteth with none save it be with them that repent and believe in his Son, who is the Holy One of Israel. (2 Nephi 30:2)

And again:

Hearken, O ye Gentiles, and hear the words of Jesus Christ, the Son of the living God, which he hath commanded me that I should speak concerning you, for, behold he commandeth me that I should write, saying: Turn, all ye Gentiles, from your wicked ways; and repent of your evil doings, of your lyings and deceivings, and of your whoredoms, and of your secret abominations, and your idolatries, and of your murders, and your priestcrafts, and your envyings, and your strifes, and from all your wickedness and abominations, and come unto me, and be baptized in my name, that ye may receive a remission of your sins, and be filled with the Holy Ghost, that ye may be numbered with my people who are of the house of Israel. (3 Nephi 30:1-2)

Over and over we are taught how straightforward the process of becoming Israel is. However, we are also taught plainly that we can choose to reject our opportunity to become a covenant people. Paul tried to convince the Hebrews that their covenant status was not guaranteed to continue despite their wickedness. He said,

I say then, Hath God cast away his people? God forbid. For I also am an Israelite, of the seed of Abraham, of the tribe of Benjamin. God hath not cast away his people which he foreknew. Wot ye not what the scripture saith of Elias? how he maketh intercession to God against Israel, saying, Lord, they have killed thy prophets, and digged down thine altars; and I am left alone, and they seek my life. But what saith the answer of God unto him? I have reserved to myself seven thousand men, who have not bowed the knee to the image of Baal. Even so then at this present time also there is a remnant according to the election of grace. And if by grace, then is it no more of works: otherwise grace is no more grace. But if it be of works, then is it no more grace: otherwise work is no more work. What then? Israel hath not obtained that which he seeketh for; but the election hath obtained it, and the rest were blinded (According as it is written, God hath given them the spirit of slumber, eyes that they should not see, and ears that they should not hear;) unto this day. And David saith, Let their table be made a snare, and a trap, and a stumblingblock, and a recompence unto them: Let their eyes be darkened, that they may not see, and bow down their back alway. I say then, Have they stumbled that they should fall? God forbid: but rather through their fall salvation is come unto the Gentiles, for to provoke them to jealousy. Now if the fall of them be the riches of the world, and the diminishing of them the riches of the Gentiles; how much more their fulness? For I speak to you Gentiles, inasmuch as I am the apostle of the Gentiles, I magnify mine office: If by any means I may provoke to emulation them which are my flesh, and might save some of them. For if the casting away of them be the reconciling of the world, what shall the receiving of them be, but life from the dead? For if the firstfruit be holy, the lump is also holy: and if the root be holy, so are the branches. And if some of the branches be broken off, and thou, being a wild olive tree, wert grafted in among them, and with them partakest of the root and fatness of the olive tree; Boast not against the branches. But if thou boast, thou bearest not the root, but the root thee. Thou wilt say then, The branches were broken off, that I might be grafted in. Well; because of unbelief they were broken off, and thou standest by faith. Be not highminded, but fear: For if God spared not the natural branches, take heed lest he also spare not thee. Behold therefore the goodness and severity of God: on them which fell, severity; but toward thee, goodness, if thou continue in his goodness: otherwise thou also shalt be cut off. And they also, if they abide not still in unbelief, shall be grafted in: for God is able to graft them in again. For if thou wert cut out of the olive tree which is wild by nature, and wert grafted contrary to nature into a good olive tree: how much more shall these, which be the natural branches, be grafted into their own olive tree? (Romans 11:1-24)

Paul taught that it was the root (the covenant connection to God through his word) that empowered the blessings of the people, not the branch (the people themselves). Paul's discourse conveys the same ideas as Jacob 5, which describes the constant process of tying in people to covenant blessings, and removing people from those blessings because of their failure to engender the works of righteousness despite the opportunity for a connection with heaven.

> Behold, I say unto you, that the house of Israel was compared unto an olive tree, by the Spirit of the Lord which was in our father; and behold are we not broken off from the house of Israel, and are we not a branch of the house of Israel? And now, the thing which our father meaneth concerning the grafting in of the natural branches through the fulness of the Gentiles, is, that in the latter days, when our seed shall have dwindled in unbelief, yea, for the space of many years, and many generations after the Messiah shall be manifested in body unto the children of men, then shall the fulness of the gospel of the Messiah come unto the Gentiles, and from the Gentiles unto the remnant of our seed— And at that day shall the remnant of our seed know that they are of the house of Israel, and that they are the covenant people of the Lord; and then shall they know and come to the knowledge of their forefathers, and also to the knowledge of the gospel of their Redeemer, which was ministered unto their fathers by him; wherefore, they shall come to the knowledge of

their Redeemer and the very points of his doctrine, that they may know how to come unto him and be saved. And then at that day will they not rejoice and give praise unto their everlasting God, their rock and their salvation? Yea, at that day, will they not receive the strength and nourishment from the true vine? Yea, will they not come unto the true fold of God? Behold, I say unto you, Yea; they shall be remembered again among the house of Israel; they shall be grafted in, being a natural branch of the olive tree, into the true olive tree. And this is what our father meaneth; and he meaneth that it will not come to pass until after they are scattered by the Gentiles; and he meaneth that it shall come by way of the Gentiles, that the Lord may show his power unto the Gentiles, for the very cause that he shall be rejected of the Jews, or of the house of Israel. (1 Nephi 15:12-17)

In our day, we choose whether we will accept the words of God, and allow ourselves to thus be grafted into the true vine, and bear choice fruit, or whether we will cut ourselves off from the true vine by stifling or refusing God's word.

Always More Word

"...for my works are without end, and also my words,
for they never cease."

–Moses 1:4

In our struggle to live the gospel of Jesus Christ, there is a constant temptation to "stick to the basics." After all, everyone struggles from time to time with those basics. Some, in fact, may be tempted to think that we have already been taught everything needed for salvation. What need is there for something more? That this attitude is antithetical to the gospel is evident in Nephi's declaration: "Wo be unto him that shall say: We have received the word of God, and we need no more of the word of God, for we have enough!"[1]

An examination of the scriptures makes clear that we do not, in fact, have everything needed for salvation. This is due to the fact that salvation cannot be offered congregationally. It always requires a personal link to God, and is predicated upon personal revelation and heed of God's word to the individual.

[1] 2 Nephi 28:29

The capstone of Nephi's teaching of faith, repentance, and baptism by water and fire is given in the end of his portion of the Book of Mormon. He says:

> And now, behold, my beloved brethren, I suppose that ye ponder somewhat in your hearts concerning that which ye should do after ye have entered in by the way. But, behold, why do ye ponder these things in your hearts? For behold, again I say unto you that if ye will enter in by the way, and receive the Holy Ghost, it will show unto you all things what ye should do. (2 Nephi 32:1,5)

If faith, repentence, and baptism were sufficient to save us, then why are we told that it is the Holy Ghost's individual teachings that will tell us what we should do? If we already know about faith in Christ, repentance, and baptism by water and fire, then what else is there to learn? Nephi is telling us that God has a lot to teach us that can only be received through the medium of individual revelation—through the Holy Ghost. Expanded personal knowledge of the doctrines of Christ are not the exception to but in fact are the very path to salvation.

> A man is saved no faster than he gets knowledge, for if he does not get knowledge, he will be brought into captivity by some evil power in the other world, as evil spirits will have more knowledge, and consequently more power than many men who are on the earth. Hence it needs revelation to assist us, and give us knowledge of the things of God. (HC 4:588)

Thus, receiving more of God's word is the key to gaining knowledge which, in turn, is the key to salvation. Consequently, he said, "It is impossible for a man to be saved in ignorance."[2] If the mysteries of God are simply tenets of doctrine that are yet unknown to the individual, and if an individual cannot be saved in ignorance, how important it is for us to seek God to learn his mysteries!

The mysteries of God—also known as the "peaceable things of the kingdom,"[3] the mysteries of God, things which cannot be written, greater things, things known by the Spirit, etc—are all the things that can be learned only directly from God. They are, in essence, the knowledge communicated to man every time God gives a dispensation of his word to an individual. Paul said these things can only be learned by the Spirit:

> For what man knoweth the things of a man, save the spirit of man which is in him? even so the things of God knoweth no man, but the Spirit of God. (1 Corinthians 2:11)

Mystery, as it is used in the scriptures, simply means anything which remains unknown to an individual. Brigham Young said, "In reality, however, there is no such thing as a mystery but to the ignorant."[4] In other words, what makes these items a mystery is not that they are unknowable, but simply that someone somewhere does not know them. Clearly, God can reveal anything to you,

---

[2] D&C 131:6
[3] D&C 36:2
[4] JD 2:90-91

and when he does, whatever he reveals ceases to be a mystery to you. At the same time, if he does not reveal that knowledge to me, it continues to be a mystery to me. There is nothing that God knows that he will not reveal to a person who seeks to know it just as soon as they are ready. "God hath not revealed anything to Joseph, but what He will make known unto the Twelve, and even the least Saint may know all things as fast as he is able to bear them."[5] There is nothing off limits. God taught very clearly that

> ...if a person gains more knowledge and intelligence in this life through his diligence and obedience than another, he will have so much the advantage in the world to come. (D&C 130:19)

So we see that what you can know in this life has nothing to do with your natural level of spirituality or the church office you may attain in this life, but everything to do with your diligence and obedience to that portion of the word of God that you have already received. God is no respecter of persons.[6] Because of this, we should expect every person on this earth can know things that very few, if any, other people know.

> For thus saith the Lord—I, the Lord, am merciful and gracious unto those who fear me, and delight to honor those who serve me in righteousness and in truth unto the end. Great shall be their reward and eternal shall be their glory. And to them will I reveal all myster-ies, yea, all the hidden mysteries of my kingdom from

---

[5] HC, 3:380
[6] D&C 38:16

days of old, and for ages to come, will I make known unto them the good pleasure of my will concerning all things pertaining to my kingdom. Yea, even the wonders of eternity shall they know, and things to come will I show them, even the things of many generations. And their wisdom shall be great, and their understanding reach to heaven; and before them the wisdom of the wise shall perish, and the understanding of the prudent shall come to naught. For by my Spirit will I enlighten them, and by my power will I make known unto them the secrets of my will—yea, even those things which eye has not seen, nor ear heard, nor yet entered into the heart of man. (D&C 76:5-10)

It should not be a rare event that certain men know things that other men do not. In fact, God promises it as a function of the Melchizedek priesthood. Therefore, everyone with the higher priesthood ought to know mysteries:

The power and authority of the higher, or Melchizedek Priesthood, is to hold the keys of all the spiritual blessings of the church—To have the privilege of receiving the mysteries of the kingdom of heaven, to have the heavens opened unto them, to commune with the general assembly and church of the Firstborn, and to enjoy the communion and presence of God the Father, and Jesus the mediator of the new covenant. (D&C 107:18-19)

God even promises the knowledge of mysteries to those without the priesthood. Here he says that all the penitent will receive mysteries that have never before been revealed, and that it will be their function and office to share those with others:

> And now behold, my brethren, what natural man is there that knoweth these things? I say unto you, there is none that knoweth these things, <u>save it be the penitent</u>. Yea, he that repenteth and exerciseth faith, and bringeth forth good works, and prayeth continually without ceasing—<u>unto such it is given to know the mysteries of God</u>; yea, unto such it shall be given to reveal things which never have been revealed; yea, and it shall be given unto such to bring thousands of souls to repentance, even as it has been given unto us to bring these our brethren to repentance. (Alma 26:22)

Because not everyone is equally penitent, we ought to expect variation in who knows what mysteries from God. We ought to expect that these mysteries are being revealed, not according to church office, but according to the humility and diligence and obedience of the individual. Humility is a real concern. <u>Pride is when individuals insist that they know more about a subject than God does.</u> You can always pinpoint these people from their conversation: "God would never..." or "that's not possible." Joseph wisely said, "I believe all that God ever revealed, and I never hear of a man being damned for believing too much; but they are damned for unbelief."[7] He said that when we box up God to

---

[7] HC 6:477

our preconceptions, we limit what he can reveal to us, damning ourselves in the process.

> [He who will not seek out or accept advanced knowledge] makes himself a fool...there is an end of his career or progress in knowledge. He cannot obtain all knowledge, for he has sealed up the gate to it. (HC 6:474-475)

Who is most likely to box God up in preconcieved notions? Who is least likely? Amongst the latter we ought to expect greater knowledge of the mysteries. Thus, we read that God:

> ...imparteth his word by angels unto men, yea, not only men but women also. Now this is not all; little children do have words given unto them many times, which confound the wise and the learned. (Alma 32:23)

And how are these mysteries made known to men? Always by a dispensation of God's word, e.g. revelation.

> For he that diligently seeketh shall find; and the mysteries of God shall be unfolded unto them, by the power of the Holy Ghost, as well in these times as in times of old, and as well in times of old as in times to come... (1 Nephi 10:19)

And again,

> Behold, great and marvelous are the works of the Lord. How unsearchable are the depths of the mysteries of him; and it is impossible that man should find out all

his ways. And no man knoweth of his ways save it be revealed unto him; wherefore, brethren, despise not the revelations of God. (Jacob 4:8)

The word of God is a fitting application for the parable of the talents told by Jesus. Each servant receives some stewardship of the word of God—his mysteries. Some bury theirs in the earth. They teach no one, they ponder not on what they've been taught, they simply ignore it. Some use what they have, exchange it with others, and obtain more to a greater or lesser degree. It is to those who use what they have and gain the most besides that the Master rewards most amply.[8]

This same lesson is repeated in the Book of Mormon. "And therefore, he that will harden his heart, the same receiveth the lesser portion of the word; and he that will not harden his heart, to him is given the greater portion of the word, until it is given unto him to know the mysteries of God until he know them in full."[9] This blessing is not received by those who claim they already have enough of God's word, and have no need or desire to learn his mysteries. God's mysteries are not some esoteric trivia about the orbit of Kolob. They are the explanation of exactly what happened in Gethsamane; they are glimpses of Jesus' life not contained in the New Testament; they are a more useful understanding of the details of certain commandments, and so on—all of which are essential for salvation. All of these mysteries are part of the codex of heaven—that which is necessary to learn in order to know God.

---

[8] See Matthew 25
[9] Alma 12:10

Our reluctance to know God is explained in some cases by a false understanding of spiritual truth. Any man will readily admit that there is enough to learn about temporal subjects that it is doubtful that any one man can know everything there is to know about a certain topic. However, we glumly assume that we can somehow master the science of God—which subsumes all temporal subjects—with one day per week of casual study. This is hardly convincing.

So how do we move away from hiding the mysteries in a napkin and toward the wise and faithful steward? Brigham Young said, "Whom shall he teach knowledge? And whom shall he make to understand doctrine? Those that are weaned from the milk and drawn from the breasts."[10] We certainly will not get to the mysteries by repeating the basics. What I am proposing is not a question of topics, mind you, but depth. There is enough to know about faith that an entire life could be consumed learning about it without reaching an end of the topic. Questions always precede instruction. A mystery is rarely revealed until after you realize you don't know it. This because God usually spends his time revealing to us the answers to our questions, and what question will you have if you feel you know everything there is to know about something? God commands us to ask questions, specifically about his mysteries:

> Ask that you may know the mysteries of God, and
> that you may translate and receive knowledge from all
> those ancient records which have been hid up, that are
> sacred; and according to your faith shall it be done

---

[10] JD 9:168

unto you. (D&C 8:11)

And again:

> Remember that without faith you can do nothing;
> therefore ask in faith. Trifle not with these things;
> do not ask for that which you ought not. Ask that
> you may know the mysteries of God, and that you may
> translate and receive knowledge from all those ancient
> records which have been hid up, that are sacred; and ac-
> cording to your faith shall it be done unto you. (D&C
> 8:10-11)

The Lord told Oliver Cowdery, "if thou wilt inquire, thou shalt know mysteries which are great and marvelous."[11] We have to have questions, and we have to petition the Lord through prayer and our own study for answers to those questions. The Lord said, "If thou shalt ask, thou shalt receive revelation upon revelation, knowledge upon knowledge, that thou mayest know the mysteries and peaceable things—that which bringeth joy, that which bringeth life eternal."[12] One scriptural example of this process is Alma, who wanted to know more about the resurrection of the dead. Said he to his son, "I show unto you one thing which I have inquired diligently of God that I might know—that is concerning the resurrection."[13] Perhaps we will come up with questions to ask on our own. If not, the Spirit will prompt us to ask the right questions. Studying the questions which prompted

[11]D&C 6:11
[12]D&C 42:61
[13]Alma 40:3

the revelations received by scriptural personalities and modern church figures will help us to learn what to ask. Studying examples of mysteries being explained in the scriptures will further our understanding of what sorts of things will be revealed to us. For example, in D&C 19, the Lord explains the mystery of his suffering in Gethsamane and the torment of the damned.

The scriptures can be a tremendous source of questions. If we trust in what others have said about certain verses, we will not have questions. However, if we toss what others have said out the window, and engage in a lively internal debate over what certain verses do or don't mean, we will find the scriptures to contain a lot more information than we previously thought. Bruce McConkie said, "Each pronouncement in the holy scriptures...is so written as to reveal little or much, depending on the spiritual capacity of the student."[14] Another mystery-killing tendency is to automatically skip over passages or phrases that do not make sense. Neal Maxwell said, "Those doctrines which may seem the most puzzling or the least attractive may well be those now most needed by us."[15] With few exceptions, it is all in there for a reason.

> Perhaps you may ask me why I dwell on this...subject. In answer, why did the Lord dwell upon it forty-two years ago, if he did not want us, in some measure, to understand it? Would he speak at random? Would he give a revelation without expecting that the people would even try to understand it? If the Lord wished us

---

[14]Bruce McConkie, "A New Witness for the Articles of Faith," Salt Lake City: Deseret Book Co., 1985, p. 71
[15]Neal Maxwell, "Notwithstanding My Weakness," p. 86

to understand something, and condescended to reveal something, why should we...think that we are stepping over our bounds in trying to comprehend approximately what the Lord desired us to understand. It is an old sectarian whim and notion, to suppose that we must not try to...understand revelation....Do not suppose, however, that those first principles [of the gospel] are the only ones to be learned; do not become stereotyped in your feelings, and think that you must always dwell upon them and proceed no further. If there be knowledge concerning the future, ...the present, ...[the] past, or any species of knowledge that would be beneficial to the mind of man, let us seek it; and that which we cannot obtain by using the light which God has placed within us, by using our reasoning powers, by reading books, or by human wisdom alone, let us seek to a higher source—to that Being who is filled with knowledge, and who has given laws to all things and who, in his wisdom, goodness, justice and mercy, controls all things according to their capacity, and according to the various spheres and conditions in which they are placed. (Orson Pratt, March 14, 1875, Salt Lake City, 16th Ward, reported by David W. Evans)

If we don't get it, or don't get why the passage was included since, in our estimation, the passage doesn't have much worth, we ought to pause and pray and go over it again. Joseph Smith said,

Men are in the habit, when the truth is exhibited by the servants of God, of saying, All is mystery; they have spoken in parables, and, therefore, are not to be understood. It is true they have eyes to see, and see not, but none are so blind as those who will not see. (TPJS, p. 96)

Questioning is how we obtain the word of God, and questioning is, therefore, the key to increasing one's faith. Remember that it was Laman and Lemuel who refused to ask questions about their father's new found religious fervor. Their implicit trust in their father was insufficient to guide them through hard times. Nephi, however, asked God. He questioned.

And it came to pass that I, Nephi, being exceedingly young, nevertheless being large in stature, and also having great desires to know of the mysteries of God, wherefore, I did cry unto the Lord; and behold he did visit me, and did soften my heart that I did believe all the words which had been spoken by my father; wherefore, I did not rebel against him like unto my brothers. And I spake unto Sam, making known unto him the things which the Lord had manifested unto me by his Holy Spirit...But, behold, Laman and Lemuel would not hearken unto my words... (1 Nephi 2:16-18)

When we make the effort to set aside our preconceived notions about what the word of God says and does not say, we will find new gems every time we read. The unbiased eyes of a convert automatically read the scriptures literally, which is how Joseph said they were intended to be read. The scriptures are full of mysteries hidden in plain sight. For example, the doctrine of the

Second Comforter, a doctrine that is treated as secret by some, sacred by others, and non-existent by still others, jumps from the pages of all the standard works when we read the verses plainly. This is why Book of Mormon personalities said that the brass plates helped them to know the mysteries of God:

> And he also taught them concerning the records which were engraven on the plates of brass, saying: My sons, I would that ye should remember that were it not for these plates, which contain these records and these commandments, we must have suffered in ignorance, even at this present time, not knowing the mysteries of God. (Mosiah 1:3)

Plain reading of God's word also dispels the negative effects of the false traditions we inherit from whatever culture we live in.

> I say unto you, my sons, were it not for [the brass plates], which have been kept and preserved by the hand of God, *that we might read and understand of his mysteries*, and have his commandments always before our eyes, that even our fathers would have dwindled in unbelief, and we should have been like unto our brethren, the Lamanites, who know nothing concerning these things, or even do not believe them when they are taught them, because of the traditions of their fathers, which are not correct. (Mosiah 1:5)

The men of God in the Book of Mormon were not bashful about God's mysteries. As indicated in the preceding quotes, it is obvious that they considered one of the prime reasons for the scriptures to be the revelation of God's mysteries to the reader. These men, like King Benjamin, frequently attempted to teach these mysteries to the audiences of their sermons:

> And these are the words which he spake and caused to be written, saying: My brethren, all ye that have assembled yourselves together, you that can hear my words which I shall speak unto you this day; for I have not commanded you to come up hither to trifle with the words which I shall speak, but that you should hearken unto me, and open your ears that ye may hear, and your hearts that ye may understand, and your minds *that the mysteries of God may be unfolded to your view.* (Mosiah 2:9)

Alma likewise taught the mysteries of God:

> Behold, he bringeth to pass the resurrection of the dead. But behold, my son, the resurrection is not yet. Now, I unfold unto you a mystery; nevertheless, there are many mysteries which are kept, that no one knoweth them save God himself. But I show unto you one thing which I have inquired diligently of God that I might know—that is concerning the resurrection. (Alma 40:3)

Joseph did the same, as do all men of God:

> I advise all to go on to perfection, and search deeper and deeper into the mysteries of Godliness....It has

always been my province to dig up hidden mysteries—
new things—for my hearers. (HC 6:363)

To these men, mysteries were not arbitrary trivia, but better understood doctrine, applicable to real life. King Benjamin would have considered his nugget about being in the service of your fellowman as service to your God a mystery. Clearly, that is a useful thing to know. Clearly, it brings us closer to Christ to practice that tenet. If we believe in a God whose words never cease, we ought to never run out of novel material to preach and teach about him, because he is always telling us something we didn't know before.

Our eventual return to the presence of God is incumbent upon our ability to receive and remain true to a greater portion of God's word direct from the heavens.

Now those men, or those women, who know no more about the power of God, and the influences of the Holy Spirit, than to be led entirely by another person, suspending their own understanding, and pinning their faith upon another's sleeve, will never be capable of entering into the celestial glory, to be crowned as they anticipate; they will never be capable of becoming Gods. They cannot rule themselves, to say nothing of ruling others, but they must be dictated to in every trifle, like a child. They cannot control themselves in the least, but James, Peter, or somebody else must control them, They never can become Gods, nor be crowned as rulers with glory, immortality, and eternal lives. They never can hold sceptres of glory, majesty, and power in the celestial kingdom. Who will? Those who are valiant and inspired with the true independence of heaven, who will go forth boldly in the service of their God, leaving others to do as they please, determined to do right, though all mankind besides should take the opposite course. (BY, JD 1:312-313)

This private dispensation of God's word always begins through the whisperings of the Holy Ghost. Eventually, however, if we remain true to what God teaches us via the First Comforter, the Holy Ghost, he will send us the Second Comforter, the presence of Christ.

...after ye had received the Holy Ghost...feast upon the words of Christ; for behold, the words of Christ will tell you all things what ye should do....if ye will enter in by the way, and receive the Holy Ghost, it will show unto you all things what ye should do. Behold, this is the doctrine of Christ, and there will be no more doctrine given until after he shall manifest himself unto you in the flesh. And when he shall manifest himself unto you in the flesh, the things which he shall say unto you shall ye observe to do. (2 Nephi 32:2-3,5-6)

The Book of Mormon contains several occurrences when Jesus fulfills the process Nephi is describing. He appears to men and teaches them things not contained in the scriptures. These are the teachings that Mormon was about to write in 3 Nephi 26:9-12, but was forbidden. These are the things that the brother of Jared saw in Ether 3:21-22 and Ether 4:1, but was forbidden to write. These teachings are described in the scriptures as "unlawful to utter."[16] These things include, but are not limited to, a vision of all things to the end of the world, and were seen by Nephi[17], John[18], the brother of Jared.[19], and Joseph Smith.[20]

Joseph explained this knowledge conveyed through the Second Comforter's visit thus:

> Now what is this other Comforter? It is no more or less than the Lord Jesus Christ himself & this is the sum & substance of the whole matter, that when any man obtains this last Comforter he will have the personage of Jesus Christ to attend him or appear unto him from time to time. & even he will manifest the Father unto him & they will take up their abode with him, & the visions of the heavens will be opened unto him & the Lord will teach him face to face & he may have a perfect knowledge of the mysteries of the kingdom of God, & this is the state & place the Ancient Saints

---

[16] 2 Corinthians 12:1-4, 3 Nephi 17:17, 3 Nephi 19:32-34, 3 Nephi 28:12-14, and D&C 76:115

[17] 1 Nephi 14:18-28

[18] 1 Nephi 14:20-22

[19] Ether 3:25

[20] "After I got through translating the Book of Mormon, I took up the Bible to read with the Urim and Thummim. I read the first chapter of Genesis and I saw the things as they were done. I turned over the next and the next, and the whole passed before me like a grand panorama; and so on chapter after chapter until I read the whole of it. I saw it all!" ("A Plainer Translation–Joseph Smith's Translation of the Bible: A History and Commentary" Matthews, Robert J., BYU Press, 1985, p 25)

arrived at when they had such glorious vision Isaiah, Ezekiel, John upon the Isle of Patmos, St Paul in the third heavens, & all the Saints who held communion with the general Assembly & Church of the First Born &c (WoJS, 27 Jun 1839)

We must have a desire to know the mysteries of God.

> For he that diligently seeketh shall find; and the mysteries of God shall be unfolded unto them, by the power of the Holy Ghost, as well in these times as in times of old, and as well in times of old as in times to come; wherefore, the course of the Lord is one eternal round.
> (1 Ne 10:19)

Nephi enjoyed many visions and revelations. Before the visions came he had "great desires to know of the mysteries of God"[21] One reason to desire to know the mysteries of God is to gain eternal life, for a knowledge of God's mysteries are essential to eternal life. "Seek not for riches but for wisdom; and, behold, the mysteries of God shall be unfolded unto you, and then shall you be made rich. Behold, he that hath eternal life is rich."[22]

Besides having a desire, asking and seeking, we must be steadfast in keeping the commandments, including those "custom commandments" which the Lord has given us through revelation. These are they whom God delights to honor with further light and truth:

---

[21] 1 Ne 2:16
[22] D&C 11:7

For thus saith the Lord—I, the Lord, am merciful and gracious unto those who fear me, and delight to honor those who serve me in righteousness and in truth unto the end. Great shall be their reward and eternal shall be their glory. And to them will I reveal all mysteries, yea, all the hidden mysteries of my kingdom from days of old, and for ages to come, will I make known unto them the good pleasure of my will concerning all things pertaining to my kingdom. Yea, even the wonders of eternity shall they know, and things to come will I show them, even the things of many generations. And their wisdom shall be great, and their understanding reach to heaven; and before them the wisdom of the wise shall perish, and the understanding of the prudent shall come to naught. For by my Spirit will I enlighten them, and by my power will I make known unto them the secrets of my will—yea, even those things which eye has not seen, nor ear heard, nor yet entered into the heart of man. (D&C 76:5-10)

And again, "But unto him that keepeth my commandments I will give the mysteries of my kingdom, and the same shall be in him a well of living water, springing up unto everlasting life."[23] The key to obtaining the mysteries of God is heeding the word of God which you have already received, and seeking more.

---

[23]D&C 62:23

Unity Through His Word

"Behold, this I have given unto you as a parable, and it
is even as I am. I say unto you, be one; and if ye are
not one ye are not mine."

–D&C 38:27

Campbellites: Unity Through Dogma

Thomas Campbell arrived in New England in 1807. His intent,
and that of his son Alexander who arrived shortly thereafter, was
to unite U.S. Christians on a common platform of New Testament
Christianity. They were strictly adherent to the text of the New
Testament. In 1824, Alexander published a series of essays entitled
"A Restoration of the Ancient Order of Things." The Campbell's
preaching yielded few conversions until they adopted a doctrinal
platform that consisted of 6 principles of conversion to Christ:
Faith, repentance, baptism for the remission of sins, the gift of
the Holy Ghost, and continuation in the doing of good works
until the end of one's life. Do these tenants look familiar? Many

Latter-day Saints mistakenly believe that Joseph's adoption of these doctrines was novel. It was not. The Campbellite platform is the same as you will here preached in LDS meetings today. You may ask what Joseph restored? Not this doctrine, as it was already restored before he arrived at Kirtland. If these tenets were the saving doctrines, what need for Joseph Smith? What then did Joseph Smith restore?

Joseph once said that all significant differences between the LDS faith and other Christian religions "were contained in the gift of the Holy Ghost."[1] Campbell did not practice laying on of hands and held that all revelation had ceased and thus the only authority was the Bible. Smith preached continuing revelation and that God's never-ceasing word empowered as it actually had historically. In other words, God's word through revelation to the individual is what makes faith in Christ living. God's living[2] word is what makes salvation possible.

The genesis and substance of Campbell's movement was that of a unity based in doctrines as preached by leadership—unity in the philosophies of men mingled with scripture. Joseph Smith's movement was unified in the belief that God gave ongoing revelation to individuals. Campbell preached a connection of men to a man (or smaller set of men) who understood the words of scripture better than everyone else. Smith preached a connection of men to heaven, where those who had made a stronger connection gave hints to those who had not.[3] Sameness is not God's unity. A military unit

---

[1] HC 4:42

[2] In hebrew, "living" is an adjective used in describing a functioning spring, which is continuously flowing.

[3] "And by so doing, the Lord God prepareth the way that the

has sameness, but of what use is it? As soon as the causing force of their unity—unrighteous dominion of men who enforce unity down the barrel of a gun—leave their ranks, pandemonium sets in. In fact, in most cases, the subordinates frequently practice all sorts of unauthorized abominations behind the back of the leader—It's all good until you are caught. This is not God's unity. Joseph said he taught correct principles and let men govern themselves.[4] God's unity is only achieved when men freely adopt the same fount of truth; when they choose to obey God.

Real Unity: God's Word

God's word is the same, thus we approach unity in command as we live the revelation of God to us as individuals. We cannot be unified or achieve God's unity if we take the arm of flesh to be our guide; policies always change. Doctrines of men will always change to match the ways of the world (though usually trailing 20 years or so behind, substituting conservatism for the unchanging righteousness of God). However, the word of God never changes. It cannot be interpreted correctly in more than one way.

> We have also a more sure word of prophecy; where-
> unto ye do well that ye take heed, as unto a light that
> shineth in a dark place, until the day dawn, and the

residue of men may have faith in Christ, that the Holy Ghost may have place in their hearts, according to the power thereof; and after this manner bringeth to pass the Father, the covenants which he hath made unto the children of men." (Moroni 7:32)

[4]Millennial Star, Nov. 15, 1851,339

day star arise in your hearts; Knowing this first, that *no prophecy of the scripture is of any private interpretation. For the prophecy came not in old time by the will of man: but holy men of God spake as they were moved by the Holy Ghost.* But there were false prophets also among the people, even as there shall be false teachers among you, who privily shall bring in damnable heresies... (2 Peter 1:19-21; 2:1)

False teachers may attempt to wrest the word of God to mean something other than was intended, but God's meaning is one. God's unity can only be attained based on the true interpretation of his word, which comes by revelation from him to us. After all, as Brigham Young taught, each of us is (or can be) an oracle of the Spirit:

This question occurred to my mind—"What causes men and women, whose minds have been unaccustomed to reflect upon theological subjects, to speak so intelligently as soon as the Spirit of the Lord touches their understanding?" The experience of most of the congregation can answer this question. You are the oracle of the Spirit, the repository of the intelligence that comes from another state of existence invisible to the natural eye; of the influence that produces an effect without revealing the cause, and is therefore called a miracle. (BY, JD 1:91)

It is only by receiving God's word directly that we can correctly interpret his written word, or that which is spoken by others. There is no way to divorce personal revelation from receiving the word of God, even if we are receiving it through others. Therefore, no written or spoken word can qualify as God's unless he himself gives us an individual connection to verify and understand it.

Thus, godly unity is not the result of a group consensus upon written or spoken doctrine, which could as easily come from men as God, and be incorrect or correct, but from a subscription to the same source of truth. Though minor differences are likely, they are not problematic. Oneness in Christ's word overlooks minor differences in belief. Joseph was exceedingly vocal about his disdain for prescription of doctrine. Consider just a few examples:

> I will endeavour to instruct you in relation to the meaning of the beasts and figures spoken of. Er (Pelatiah) Brown has been the cause of this subject being now presented before you. He, is one of the wisest old heads we have among us, has been called up before the High Council on account of the beast. The old man has preached concerning the beast which was full of eyes before and behind and for this he was hauled up for trial. I never thought it was right to call up a man and try him because he erred in doctrine, it looks too much like methodism and not like Latter day Saintism. Methodists have creeds which a man must believe or be kicked out of their church. I want the liberty of believing as I please, it feels so good not to be tramelled. It dont prove that a man is not a good man, because he errs in doctrine. The High Council undertook to censure and correct Er Brown because of his teachings in relation to the beasts, and he came to me to know

what he should do about it. (Words of Joseph Smith, 8 April 1843)

And again,

> [some] have creeds which a man must believe or be asked out of their church. I want the liberty of thinking and believing as I please, it feels so good not to be trammeled. It does not prove that a man is not a good man because he errs in doctrine. (HC 5:340)

And again,

> I ask did I ever exerise any compulsion over any man. did I not give him the liberty of disbelieveing any doctrin I have preached if he saw fit? (Words of Joseph Smith, 24 Mar 1844)

When we subscribe to God's word, we change.

> And the Father and I are one. I am in the Father and the Father in me; and inasmuch as ye have received me, ye are in me and I in you. (D&C 50:43)

As we achieve a more steadfast devotion to God's unchanging perfection, our changing mind and will brings us closer to those around us who have similarly subscribed to God's word. To the degree that we seek and heed God's word, we become like him. Jesus obtained his word in full, and therefore become completely like the Father: completely unified with him through sharing his knowledge and attributes:

> And that I am in the Father, and the Father in me, and
> the Father and I are one—The Father because he gave
> me of his fulness, and the Son because I was in the
> world and made flesh my tabernacle, and dwelt among
> the sons of men. I was in the world and received of
> my Father, and the works of him were plainly manifest.
> (D&C 93:3-5)

Our incorporation of God's word into ourselves is how he dwells
in us and how his power is manifested through us, just like it was
in Jesus. When he came as a man, he gave the perfect example as
a man. "And every one that hearkeneth to the voice of the Spirit
cometh unto God, even the Father."[5] Seeking and heeding his
word brings us closer to Him because it makes us one with him.

> Believest thou not that I am in the Father, and the
> Father in me? the words that I speak unto you I speak
> not of myself: but the Father that dwelleth in me, he
> doeth the works. Believe me that I am in the Father,
> and the Father in me: or else believe me for the very
> works' sake. (John 14:10-11)

Though all of us will proceed line upon line, and thus will have
perhaps vast swaths of subjects that have not yet been revealed to
us upon which we may disagree, as a whole we will rejoice and
unify in our objective to come closer to Christ through obtaining
and living God's word. Thus we become one with the Son, one
with the Father, and one with all others who are seeking Christ.

---

[5]D&C 84:47

"Behold, this I have given unto you as a parable, and it is even as I am. I say unto you, be one; and if ye are not one ye are not mine."[6]

Unity in God's House

God told Alma that his church was composed of "he that will hear my voice."[7] The Lord's house is all those who seek, obtain, and heed his word. By definition, this house is ordered because it is composed of those who obey God's orders—his word.

> "Behold, mine house is a house of order, saith the Lord God, and not a house of confusion. Will I accept of an offering, saith the Lord, that is not made in my name? Or will I receive at your hands that which I have not appointed? And will I appoint unto you, saith the Lord, except it be by law, even as I and my Father ordained unto you, before the world was? (D&C 132: 8-11)

Note that men are not a part of this equation, except and unless their words are received explicitly from God. His appointments, which are his word, are what order his house. By definition, his word in the scriptures is the foundational source for this order. Any deviations from his word must necessarily come from his

---

[6] D&C 38:27

[7] "And he that will hear my voice shall be my sheep; and him shall ye receive into the church, and him will I also receive. For behold, this is my church; whosoever is baptized shall be baptized unto repentance. And whomsoever ye receive shall believe in my name; and him will I freely forgive." (Mosiah 26:21-22)

own mouth, such as when he commanded Nephi to divert from the command, "thou shalt not kill" and slay Laban. We find ample examples of men ordering God's house through preaching his word in the scriptures. For example, Alma went forth to divorce the church from their false notions and thus order it by preaching the word of God.

> And this he did that he himself might go forth among his people, or among the people of Nephi, that he might preach the word of God unto them, to stir them up in remembrance of their duty, and that he might pull down, by the word of God, all the pride and craftiness and all the contentions which were among his people, seeing no way that he might reclaim them save it were in bearing down in pure testimony against them. (Alma 4:19)

An example of what he taught is found in Alma chapters 5 and 6. The Lord tells us that at some point the Lord will send a servant to put the house of God in order once again. Some consider this prophesy to be fulfilled, though it is clear that such is not the case since at least one critical item (to give lands of inheritance to the Saints) has not occurred.

> And it shall come to pass that I, the Lord God, will send one mighty and strong, holding the scepter of power in his hand, clothed with light for a covering, whose mouth shall utter words, eternal words; while his bowels shall be a fountain of truth, to set in order

the house of God, and to arrange by lot the inheri-
tances of the saints whose names are found, and the
names of their fathers, and of their children, enrolled
in the book of the law of God; (D&C 85:7)

At any rate, we can rest assured that when God sets about to order
his house again, he will do it according to the pattern he has
always followed: His servant will preach God's word.

Though surface sameness can be achieved by unrighteous dominion of men, Zion cannot be built upon this principle. Unity
in heart and mind, which Zion necessitates, can only be achieved
when men choose to obey God's word. "And the Lord called his
people Zion, because they were of one heart and one mind, and
dwelt in righteousness; and there was no poor among them."[8] If
all men took the word of God as their guide, we would have unity
indeed.

---

[8]Moses 7:18

Like Unto Moses

"Wherefore, I, Nephi, did exhort them to give heed
unto the word of the Lord; yea, I did exhort them
with all the energies of my soul, and with all the
faculty which I possessed, that they would give heed to
the word of God and remember to keep his
commandments always in all things."

–1 Nephi 15:25

1 Nephi 17 provides a case study to the importance of seeking, obtaining, and following God's word.

The chapter begins describing their sojourn in the wilderness:

> 1 And it came to pass that we did again take our journey in the wilderness; and we did travel nearly eastward from that time forth. And we did travel and wade through much affliction in the wilderness; and our women did bear children in the wilderness.
>
> 2 And so great were the blessings of the Lord upon us, that while we did live upon raw meat in the wilderness,

our women did give plenty of suck for their children, and were strong, yea, even like unto the men; and they began to bear their journeyings without murmurings.

3 And thus we see that the commandments of God must be fulfilled. And if it so be that the children of men keep the commandments of God he doth nourish them, and strengthen them, and provide means whereby they can accomplish the thing which he has commanded them; wherefore, he did provide means for us while we did sojourn in the wilderness.

4 And we did sojourn for the space of many years, yea, even eight years in the wilderness.

Note that Nephi is explicit in identifying that their journey in the wilderness was prescribed by God's word. It is also interesting that the presence of God's power is completely linked to the accomplishment of his command. In other words, one might wonder, would God had given them nourishment, strength, and means if they were not in the process of fulfilling his instructions? So often we consider "keeping the commandments" as a sidebar status to everyday life—an addendum to business as usual. If we are maintaining the Lord's standards, he will infuse his blessings and power into our life, with *our* being emphasized. This is not how it works. Nephi had to seek for God to dictate instruction to him. Then, he sought to live the instruction. Power was not infused into Nephi's life—Nephi course corrected his life into the stream of God's work, where his power dwells.

5 And we did come to the land which we called Boun-

tiful, because of its much fruit and also wild honey; and all these things were prepared of the Lord that we might not perish. And we beheld the sea, which we called Irreantum, which, being interpreted, is many waters.

6 And it came to pass that we did pitch our tents by the seashore; and notwithstanding we had suffered many afflictions and much difficulty, yea, even so much that we cannot write them all, we were exceedingly rejoiced when we came to the seashore; and we called the place Bountiful, because of its much fruit.

7 And it came to pass that after I, Nephi, had been in the land of Bountiful for the space of many days, the voice of the Lord came unto me, saying: Arise, and get thee into the mountain. And it came to pass that I arose and went up into the mountain, and cried unto the Lord.

Nephi is given instruction here without even asking. By following it, he receives more. Light cleaves to light. Instruction to instruction. What if Nephi had ignored this invitation to go to the mountain? He surely would not have had the following experience. The word of the Lord is always dispensed in waves, with greater light and truth given to those who heed the previous instructions.

8 And it came to pass that the Lord spake unto me, saying: Thou shalt construct a ship, after the manner

which I shall show thee, that I may carry thy people across these waters.

9 And I said: Lord, whither shall I go that I may find ore to molten, that I may make tools to construct the ship after the manner which thou hast shown unto me?

10 And it came to pass that the Lord told me whither I should go to find ore, that I might make tools.

Again we see that the proportion of revelation handily increases as individuals shift into the Lord's service. By following a simple and brief instruction to go pray, Nephi received great instruction to build a ship and had the opportunity to ask God questions about the task he had been given and receive a response. It it interesting to consider whether Nephi would have been so readily answered by the Lord in his prayers if he had shirked the Lord's invitation to accept a special mission. In other words, it is almost surely the case that Nephi's prayers while on the Lord's errand were much more conversational with the Lord than those while on his own errand. And so it is.

11 And it came to pass that I, Nephi, did make a bellows wherewith to blow the fire, of the skins of beasts; and after I had made a bellows, that I might have wherewith to blow the fire, I did smite two stones together that I might make fire.

12 For the Lord had not hitherto suffered that we should make much fire, as we journeyed in the wilderness; for he said: I will make thy food become sweet, that ye cook it not;

13 And I will also be your light in the wilderness; and I will prepare the way before you, if it so be that ye shall keep my commandments; wherefore, inasmuch as ye shall keep my commandments ye shall be led towards the promised land; and ye shall know that it is by me that ye are led.

14 Yea, and the Lord said also that: After ye have arrived in the promised land, ye shall know that I, the Lord, am God; and that I, the Lord, did deliver you from destruction; yea, that I did bring you out of the land of Jerusalem.

15 Wherefore, I, Nephi, did strive to keep the commandments of the Lord, and I did exhort my brethren to faithfulness and diligence.

16 And it came to pass that I did make tools of the ore which I did molten out of the rock.

And thus we see the implicit passage of time in these verses. God can reveal tremendous things to a person, and then stay mostly quiet for a long time. We are given enough instructions to keep us moving forward, and there really isn't much need of follow up until we have accomplished what he has told us to do.

17 And when my brethren saw that I was about to build a ship, they began to murmur against me, saying: Our brother is a fool, for he thinketh that he can build a ship; yea, and he also thinketh that he can cross these great waters.

18 And thus my brethren did complain against me, and were desirous that they might not labor, for they did not believe that I could build a ship; neither would they believe that I was instructed of the Lord.

19 And now it came to pass that I, Nephi, was exceedingly sorrowful because of the hardness of their hearts; and now when they saw that I began to be sorrowful they were glad in their hearts, insomuch that they did rejoice over me, saying: We knew that ye could not construct a ship, for we knew that ye were lacking in judgment; wherefore, thou canst not accomplish so great a work.

20 And thou art like unto our father, led away by the foolish imaginations of his heart; yea, he hath led us out of the land of Jerusalem, and we have wandered in the wilderness for these many years; and our women have toiled, being big with child; and they have borne children in the wilderness and suffered all things, save it were death; and it would have been better that they had died before they came out of Jerusalem than to have suffered these afflictions.

21 Behold, these many years we have suffered in the wilderness, which time we might have enjoyed our possessions and the land of our inheritance; yea, and we might have been happy.

22 And we know that the people who were in the land of Jerusalem were a righteous people; for they

kept the statutes and judgments of the Lord, and all his commandments, according to the law of Moses; wherefore, we know that they are a righteous people; and our father hath judged them, and hath led us away because we would hearken unto his words; yea, and our brother is like unto him. And after this manner of language did my brethren murmur and complain against us.

There is opposition in all things. The opposition to the mission Nephi had been given came, notably, after much time had passed from when Nephi received God's word on the subject. When we are first told something by God, it is the most important thing in our mind. However, with the passage of time, it can be choked out by the cares of the world. As Jesus taught, "He also that received seed among the thorns is he that heareth the word; and the care of this world, and the deceitfulness of riches, choke the word, and he becometh unfruitful."[1] This is why it is always a good idea to keep a journal of the Lord's dealings with you.

> 23 And it came to pass that I, Nephi, spake unto them, saying: Do ye believe that our fathers, who were the children of Israel, would have been led away out of the hands of the Egyptians if they had not hearkened unto the words of the Lord?
>
> 24 Yea, do ye suppose that they would have been led out of bondage, if the Lord had not commanded Moses that he should lead them out of bondage?

---

[1] Matthew 13:22

25 Now ye know that the children of Israel were in bondage; and ye know that they were laden with tasks, which were grievous to be borne; wherefore, ye know that it must needs be a good thing for them, that they should be brought out of bondage.

26 Now ye know that Moses was commanded of the Lord to do that great work; and ye know that by his word the waters of the Red Sea were divided hither and thither, and they passed through on dry ground.

27 But ye know that the Egyptians were drowned in the Red Sea, who were the armies of Pharaoh.

28 And ye also know that they were fed with manna in the wilderness.

29 Yea, and ye also know that Moses, by his word according to the power of God which was in him, smote the rock, and there came forth water, that the children of Israel might quench their thirst.

30 And notwithstanding they being led, the Lord their God, their Redeemer, going before them, leading them by day and giving light unto them by night, and doing all things for them which were expedient for man to receive, they hardened their hearts and blinded their minds, and reviled against Moses and against the true and living God.

31 And it came to pass that according to his word he did destroy them; and according to his word he did lead them; and according to his word he did do all

things for them; and there was not any thing done save it were by his word.

32 And after they had crossed the river Jordan he did make them mighty unto the driving out of the children of the land, yea, unto the scattering them to destruction.

33 And now, do ye suppose that the children of this land, who were in the land of promise, who were driven out by our fathers, do ye suppose that they were righteous? Behold, I say unto you, Nay.

34 Do ye suppose that our fathers would have been more choice than they if they had been righteous? I say unto you, Nay.

35 Behold, the Lord esteemeth all flesh in one; he that is righteous is favored of God. But behold, this people had rejected every word of God, and they were ripe in iniquity; and the fulness of the wrath of God was upon them; and the Lord did curse the land against them, and bless it unto our fathers; yea, he did curse it against them unto their destruction, and he did bless it unto our fathers unto their obtaining power over it.

36 Behold, the Lord hath created the earth that it should be inhabited; and he hath created his children that they should possess it.

37 And he raiseth up a righteous nation, and destroyeth the nations of the wicked.

38 And he leadeth away the righteous into precious

lands, and the wicked he destroyeth, and curseth the land unto them for their sakes.

39 He ruleth high in the heavens, for it is his throne, and this earth is his footstool.

40 And he loveth those who will have him to be their God. Behold, he loved our fathers, and he covenanted with them, yea, even Abraham, Isaac, and Jacob; and he remembered the covenants which he had made; wherefore, he did bring them out of the land of Egypt.

41 And he did straiten them in the wilderness with his rod; for they hardened their hearts, even as ye have; and the Lord straitened them because of their iniquity. He sent fiery flying serpents among them; and after they were bitten he prepared a way that they might be healed; and the labor which they had to perform was to look; and because of the simpleness of the way, or the easiness of it, there were many who perished.

42 And they did harden their hearts from time to time, and they did revile against Moses, and also against God; nevertheless, ye know that they were led forth by his matchless power into the land of promise.

43 And now, after all these things, the time has come that they have become wicked, yea, nearly unto ripeness; and I know not but they are at this day about to be destroyed; for I know that the day must surely come that they must be destroyed, save a few only, who shall be led away into captivity.

44 Wherefore, the Lord commanded my father that he should depart into the wilderness; and the Jews also sought to take away his life; yea, and ye also have sought to take away his life; wherefore, ye are murderers in your hearts and ye are like unto them.

45 Ye are swift to do iniquity but slow to remember the Lord your God. Ye have seen an angel, and he spake unto you; yea, ye have heard his voice from time to time; and he hath spoken unto you in a still small voice, but ye were past feeling, that ye could not feel his words; wherefore, he has spoken unto you like unto the voice of thunder, which did cause the earth to shake as if it were to divide asunder.

46 And ye also know that by the power of his almighty word he can cause the earth that it shall pass away; yea, and ye know that by his word he can cause the rough places to be made smooth, and smooth places shall be broken up. O, then, why is it, that ye can be so hard in your hearts?

47 Behold, my soul is rent with anguish because of you, and my heart is pained; I fear lest ye shall be cast off forever. Behold, I am full of the Spirit of God, insomuch that my frame has no strength.

When we are tried in our faithfulness to God's instruction to us, we are apt to recognize our own weakness and inadequacy to the assigned task. However, like Nephi, we will gain strength in the Lord when we consider and remember the examples of God's servants before us, who, notwithstanding their weakness, were made strong inasmuch as they humbled themselves and did what God told them to do.

> 48 And now it came to pass that when I had spoken these words they were angry with me, and were desirous to throw me into the depths of the sea; and as they came forth to lay their hands upon me I spake unto them, saying: In the name of the Almighty God, I command you that ye touch me not, for I am filled with the power of God, even unto the consuming of my flesh; and whoso shall lay his hands upon me shall wither even as a dried reed; and he shall be as naught before the power of God, for God shall smite him.

Would Nephi have received God's power of protection if his brothers were not about to attempt to kill him? Suppose his sermon on remembering their fathers had been successful. Would there have been a need? God's power is always reserved for God's purposes. It is not to be used, even by those who have it, haphazardly.

> 49 And it came to pass that I, Nephi, said unto them that they should murmur no more against their father; neither should they withhold their labor from me, for God had commanded me that I should build a ship.

> 50 And I said unto them: If God had commanded me to do all things I could do them. If he should command me that I should say unto this water, be thou

earth, it should be earth; and if I should say it, it would be done.

In perhaps the best explanation of priesthood power, Nephi explains that a person encounters God's power when that person encounter's God's invitation. Whatever the individual is asked to do, he receives power to do.

51 And now, if the Lord has such great power, and has wrought so many miracles among the children of men, how is it that he cannot instruct me, that I should build a ship?

52 And it came to pass that I, Nephi, said many things unto my brethren, insomuch that they were confounded and could not contend against me; neither durst they lay their hands upon me nor touch me with their fingers, even for the space of many days. Now they durst not do this lest they should wither before me, so powerful was the Spirit of God; and thus it had wrought upon them.

53 And it came to pass that the Lord said unto me: Stretch forth thine hand again unto thy brethren, and they shall not wither before thee, but I will shock them, saith the Lord, and this will I do, that they may know that I am the Lord their God.

54 And it came to pass that I stretched forth my hand unto my brethren, and they did not wither before me; but the Lord did shake them, even according to the word which he had spoken.

55 And now, they said: We know of a surety that the Lord is with thee, for we know that it is the power of the Lord that has shaken us. And they fell down before me, and were about to worship me, but I would not suffer them, saying: I am thy brother, yea, even thy younger brother; wherefore, worship the Lord thy God, and honor thy father and thy mother, that thy days may be long in the land which the Lord thy God shall give thee.

Whereas God's voice is absent from this encounter from the moment of rebellion until now, God now intercedes to instruct Nephi on how he will be merciful to them and how he will exercise his power on Nephi's behalf. It is interesting that God allows Nephi to say and do what he has done to this point based upon his knowledge of the mind and will of God.

The Words of Eternal Life

"Then Simon Peter answered him, Lord, to whom
shall we go? thou hast the words of eternal life."

–John 6:68

The Lord Jesus Christ has been empowered by the Father to
seal individuals up to eternal life. This process is called having
your calling and election made sure. Peter was, in one sense,
referring to the Savior's promise of eternal life when he said that
the Savior had the words of eternal life. That his statement is also
true in a broader sense is evident when you consider that the only
way an individual obtains and fulfills that promise is by following
the other words of Christ.[1] The Lord said that "He that heareth
my word, and believeth on him that sent me, hath everlasting life,
and shall not come into condemnation; but is passed from death

---

[1] For example, consider what the Lord told Oliver: "Behold,
thou art Oliver, and I have spoken unto thee because of thy desires;
therefore treasure up these words in thy heart. Be faithful and
diligent in keeping the commandments of God, and I will encircle
thee in the arms of my love." (D&C 6:20)

unto life."[2]

The Lord revealed to us the process of obtaining the words of eternal life:

> And I now give unto you a commandment to beware concerning yourselves, to give diligent heed to the words of eternal life. For you shall live by every word that proceedeth forth from the mouth of God. For the word of the Lord is truth, and whatsoever is truth is light, and whatsoever is light is Spirit, even the Spirit of Jesus Christ. And the Spirit giveth light to every man that cometh into the world; and the Spirit enlighteneth every man through the world, that hearkeneth to the voice of the Spirit. And every one that hearkeneth to the voice of the Spirit cometh unto God, even the Father. And the Father teacheth him of the covenant which he has renewed and confirmed upon you, which is confirmed upon you for your sakes, and not for your sakes only, but for the sake of the whole world. (D&C 84:43-48)

The Father is the one who possesses the words of eternal life. That collection of his word is delivered through Jesus Christ[3] (and optionally through angels and men) to us line upon line to the degree that we receive it. As we infuse those words into our spirit by receiving them, and then subdue our bodies to obey them, we

---

[2] John 5:24

[3] He that loveth me not keepeth not my sayings: and the word which ye hear is not mine, but the Father's which sent me. (John 14:24)

rise to another plane of existence. When followed to the end, this process always ends with eternal life.[4]

Codex of Heaven and One Eternal Round

The word of God is not a divine quote book of things that God happens to have said by chance. The course of God is one eternal round.[5] What does this mean? Our phase of the plan of salvation, beginning with the fall of Adam and ending with Christ turning over the subdued creation to Heavenly Father, is a set of circumstances that can be viewed as a station in an automated factory. Every widget that comes across the belt is subjected to the same exact process. In this case, the robot is God, and the current Heavenly Father will be replaced by his successor, Jesus Christ, at the end of this round, who will do exactly what his Father did before him. Consider the following verses. "Listen to the voice of the Lord your God, even Alpha and Omega, the beginning and the end, whose course is one eternal round, the same today as yesterday, and forever."[6] Why is "he" the same today, yesterday,

---

[4]"It was the credence they gave to the testimony of their fathers—this testimony having aroused their minds to inquire after the knowledge of God. The inquiry frequently terminated, indeed, always terminated when rightly pursued, in the most glorious discoveries and eternal certainty." (Lectures on Faith 2:56)

[5]And it may suffice if I only say they are preserved for a wise purpose, which purpose is known unto God; for he doth counsel in wisdom over all his works, and his paths are straight, and his course is one eternal round.(Alma 37:12)

[6]D&C 35:1

and forever? Well, whoever is in his role does the same thing in our course (our phase of the plan of salvation) without deviation. There is no other way to bring matter in a pre-existent state of organization to matter in the state of exaltation. As we are told, the plan is pre-defined:

> For God doth not walk in crooked paths, neither doth he turn to the right hand nor to the left, neither doth he vary from that which he hath said, therefore his paths are straight, and his course is one eternal round. (D&C 3:2)

And again,

> I perceive that it has been made known unto you, by the testimony of his word, that he cannot walk in crooked paths; neither doth he vary from that which he hath said; neither hath he a shadow of turning from the right to the left, or from that which is right to that which is wrong; therefore, his course is one eternal round. (Alma 7:20)

Nephi explains this process duplisitically:

> For he that diligently seeketh shall find; and the mysteries of God shall be unfolded unto them, by the power of the Holy Ghost, as well in these times as in times of old, and as well in times of old as in times to come; wherefore, the course of the Lord is one eternal round. (1 Nephi 10:19)

Nephi's reasoning fits ancient times of old in the earthy scope as well as pre-existent times, and times to come on earth as well as times to come after earth.

The ascent of Gods is iterative. Each iteration of what we know as the creation is the same. Jesus said that "...the Son can do nothing of himself, but what he seeth the Father do: for what things soever he doeth, these also doeth the Son likewise."[7] Joseph, remarking about this verse, said,

> What did Jesus do? Why, I do the things I saw my Father do when worlds came rolling into existence. My Father worked out His kingdom with fear and trembling, and I must do the same; and when I get my kingdom, I shall present it to my Father, so that He may obtain kingdom upon kingdom, and it will exalt Him in glory. He will then take a higher exaltation, and I will take His place, and thereby become exalted myself. (HC 6:306)

So the Son treads the path of the Father. This is why Jesus could be told everything he would have to do as the Savior. This is how Satan knew ahead of time that Adam and Eve had to partake of the fruit as "on other worlds." Having proven that future iterations are repetitive, we must still show that past ones were as well. Abraham wrote,

> ...the Lord said unto me: These two facts do exist, that there are two spirits, one being more intelligent than

---

[7]John 5:19

the other; there shall be another more intelligent than they; I am the Lord thy God, I am more intelligent than they all. (Abraham 3:19)

Commenting on this verse, Joseph remarked:

[Suppose we have] two men on the earth, one wiser than the other, [that] would logically show that another who is wiser than the wisest may exist. Intelligences exist one above another, so that there is no end to them. (HC 6:476)

He explained,

If Jesus Christ was the Son of God, and John discovered that God the Father of Jesus Christ had a Father, you may suppose that He had a Father also. Where was there ever a son without a father? And where was there ever a father without first being a son?....If Jesus had a Father, can we not believe He had a Father also? (HC 6:476)

This is why the Lord's course is one eternal round.

With this definition of "one eternal round" in mind, it becomes clear that the word of God is a finite set of words that compose God's law in our present scope of existence. They are not only non-arbitrary, but they are pre-defined, like an instruction manual for this phase of the creation. The words that the Father speaks and that the son is given to speak are exactly the same in every iteration of creation. This is why Joseph could speak of the revelations being a "transcript from the records of the eternal world."[8] The record of the eternal world is the codex of the word of God for our phase of this iteration of creation. Angels speak by the power of the Holy Ghost and the Holy Ghost is the record of heaven. God's word to us consists of excerpts from that record.[9]

Besides the scriptural references to the eternal round, we have another evidence for the heavenly codex concept in a teaching from Joseph Smith. He taught that God had the foreknowledge to know exactly what to reveal to men:

> The God of heaven understanding most perfectly the constitution of human nature, and the weakness of men, knew what was necessary to be revealed, and what ideas must be planted in their minds in order that they might be enabled to exercise faith in him unto eternal life. (Lectures on Faith 4:2)

---

[8]Joseph said about D&C 76: "Nothing could be more pleasing to the Saints upon the order of the kingdom of the Lord, than the light which burst upon the world through the foregoing vision. Every law, every commandment, every promise, every truth, and every point touching the destiny of man, from Genesis to Revelation, where the purity of the scriptures remains unsullied by the folly of men, go to show the perfection of the theory [of different degrees of glory in the future life] and witnesses the fact that that document is a transcript from the records of the eternal world." (HC 1:252-253)

[9]The use of the word "record" here is the same as used by Joseph Smith who referred to the Book of Mormon as a record. It is not used in the sense of a recording of acts on earth.

A strong witness to this principle is found in observations about the words of both angels and prophets. We find that angels, whenever they appear, speak scripture. Why is that? Why does God choose to repeat himself? Why does Christ himself quote scripture when he appears, as he did to Joseph, the Nephites, and all through his mortal ministry to the Jews? It is because the scriptures are not the work of the writers. Inasmuch as they are the word of God, they are merely quotes from the record of heaven. In other words, Jesus, angels, and prophets are all citing the same "book." For this reason, we get almost identical scriptures given by prophets who never interacted with each other. Jesus gives the same sermon to both the Jews and the Nephites. Micah and Isaiah speak of the "mountain of the Lord's house." Mormon and Paul give almost the exact same observations about faith.[10] This pattern goes on and on:

---

[10]See 1 Corinthians 13 and Moroni 7

And now also the axe is laid unto the root of the trees: therefore every tree which bringeth not forth good fruit is hewn down, and cast into the fire. (Matthew 3:10)

And again I say unto you, the Spirit saith: Behold, the ax is laid at the root of the tree; therefore every tree that bringeth not forth good fruit shall be hewn down and cast into the fire, yea, a fire which cannot be consumed, even an unquenchable fire. Behold, and remember, the Holy One hath spoken it. (Alma 5:52)

Therefore, my beloved brethren, be ye steadfast, unmoveable, always abounding in the work of the Lord, forasmuch as ye know that your labour is not in vain in the Lord. (1 Corinthians 15:58)

Therefore, I would that ye should be steadfast and immovable, always abounding in good works, that Christ, the Lord God Omnipotent, may seal you his, that you may be brought to heaven, that ye may have everlasting salvation and eternal life, through the wisdom, and power, and justice, and mercy of him who created all things, in heaven and in earth, who is God above all. Amen. (Mosiah 5:15)

For, behold, the day cometh, that shall burn as an oven; and all the proud, yea, and all that do wickedly, shall be stubble: and the day that cometh shall burn them up, saith the Lord of hosts, that it shall leave them neither root nor branch. (Malachi 4:1)

For behold, saith the prophet, the time cometh speedily that Satan shall have no more power over the hearts of the children of men; for the day soon cometh that all the proud and they who do wickedly shall be as stubble; and the day cometh that they must be burned. (1 Nephi 22:15)

For to one is given by the Spirit the word of wisdom; to another the word of knowledge by the same Spirit; To another faith by the same Spirit; to another the gifts of healing by the same Spirit; To another the working of miracles; to another prophecy; to another discerning of spirits; to another divers kinds of tongues; to another the interpretation of tongues: But all these worketh that one and the selfsame Spirit, dividing to every man severally as he will.(1 Corinthians 12)

For behold, to one is given by the Spirit of God, that he may teach the word of wisdom; And to another, that he may teach the word of knowledge by the same Spirit; And to another, exceedingly great faith; and to another, the gifts of healing by the same Spirit; And again, to another, that he may work mighty miracles; And again, to another, that he may prophesy concerning all things; (Moroni 10)

Opponents would claim that these scriptures are examples of plagiarism. They are right, but not in the way they intend. The words are all taken from the same source—the record of heaven.

The idea that God's word consists of an explicit codex that is the same from eternal round to eternal round and consists of everything necessary for salvation ought to give us pause. It ought to add to the significance of what God has already said to us, say, in the scriptures. It ought to add to the distinction that we can make between the words of God and the words of men, and show that they are not interchangable or even comparable due, if for no other reason, to their genesis.

However, there is a deeper difference, which makes more significant the need for God to know what words are necessary for us to secure eternal life. Let us consider the effects of the word of God on the soul.

Effect of Word on the Soul

Jesus said, "It is the spirit that quickeneth; the flesh profiteth nothing: the words that I speak unto you, they are spirit, and they are life."[11] Jesus did not say that the words *bring* life. He said they *are* life. He also said they are spirit. That which is spirit is light and truth. "For the word of the Lord is truth, and whatsoever is truth is light, and whatsoever is light is Spirit, even the Spirit of

---

[11]John 6:63

Jesus Christ."[12] When we seek, obtain, and absorb the light and truth that is the word of God, our being undergoes a change. It is infused with light and truth. It is infused with the spirit of Christ. It becomes the oracle of God in us. It allows us to become part of God and God part of us.

Our spirit is an access point for supernatural influence, whether good or evil. God's influence comes through the Holy Ghost. Satan's comes through the flesh. The access point for both is our spirit. When we hearken to the word of God, our spirits become Holy, and this can sanctify the flesh. When we hearken to the devil, our spirits become sullied and are overcome by our flesh. Hence Jesus said, "It is the spirit that quickeneth; the flesh profiteth nothing: the words that I speak unto you, they are spirit, and they are life."[13]

Quickening is the effect of God's spirit through our spirit on our flesh. The purpose of this life is for us to subdue our bodies to the influence of God's word through our spirit.

> For the natural man is an enemy to God, and has been from the fall of Adam, and will be, forever and ever, unless he yields to the enticings of the Holy Spirit, and putteth off the natural man and becometh a saint through the atonement of Christ the Lord, and becometh as a child, submissive, meek, humble, patient, full of love, willing to submit to all things which the Lord seeth fit to inflict upon him, even as a child doth submit to his father. (Mosiah 3:19)

---

[12]D&C 84:45
[13]John 6:63

The spirit can exalt the body if the body is subdued to the spirit by bringing the flesh to the level of glory enjoyed by the spirit prior to this life. The spirit, beginning life as more refined matter, can serve as an injection point for the word of God into the flesh, which is made of fallen material and is of a lower glory than the spirit. Death is the effect of the devil's influence through our bodies on our spirits. When we succumb to the devil's temptations to our flesh, we bring down our spirits to the fallen degree of our bodies. This process is illustrated in those disembodied spirits who, during life, embraced their carnal addictions and thus find themselves, in spirit, suffering from the carnal desires that plagued them in the flesh. There are only two types of beings: the quick and the dead.[14] The quick are those who are actuated by God's word. The dead are those who are not. Thus, "to be carnally minded is death; but to be spiritually minded is life and peace."[15]

Spirits good and bad infuse their qualities upon us when we embrace them. Evil spirits act upon our flesh to imprint their devilish desires upon our spirits, which exercise control upon our bodies. The medium of this effect is the word of the evil one or his imps. The spirit of God acts upon our spirits to imprint the mind and will of God upon us, empowering us to use our spirits to do the same to our bodies. The medium for this effect is the word of God. The word of God sanctifies us as we infuse it into our soul. These two warring influences provide us opposition in all things. To win the war, we must hearken to God's word.

And I said unto them that it was the word of God;

---

[14]See Moroni 10:34.
[15]Romans 8:6; See also 2 Nephi 9:39.

and whoso would hearken unto the word of God, and would hold fast unto it, they would never perish; neither could the temptations and the fiery darts of the adversary overpower them unto blindness, to lead them away to destruction. (1 Nephi 15:24)

Jesus asked the Father to "Sanctify them through thy truth: thy word is truth."[16] He also declared the apostles "clean through the word which I have spoken unto you."[17] Jesus described how his word purifies us as we have faith in it.[18]

Quickening and sanctification, two synonyms for the same process, is gradual. Two analogies used in scripture to describe this process are leavening and grafting. God's word is like leaven in dough. The bacteria infused in leavened dough multiply and take over the whole lump of dough. Despite the initial paucity of leaven, if the process is continued under the right conditions, it will eventually take over the entire lump. Grafting occurs when God imbues in us a portion of his word. The hope is that the graft will change the entire tree to produce the same type of fruit as the graft produces. The graft changes the tree into itself. Christ is the true vine, and in order to be saved we must be grafted into him. No one can be saved until and unless they become like Christ. They must be able to say, as Christ did, I am in the Father and the

---

[16]John 17:17

[17]John 15:3

[18]"Father, I thank thee that thou hast purified those whom I have chosen, because of their faith, and I pray for them, and also for them who shall believe on their words, that they may be purified in me, through faith on their words, even as they are purified in me." (3 Nephi 19:28)

Father is in me. When we are grafted into him, his word flows through us and is found in us. We bear fruit. The juice of grapes is the color of blood. We drink the blood of Christ symbolically in the sacrament. Blood flows through the umbilical cord to a baby. As the word flows through us and is found in us, we are sanctified by the blood of Jesus. While justification is the forgiveness of our sins, sanctification is the process of becoming like God in heart, mind, and strength.

> That by reason of transgression cometh the fall, which fall bringeth death, and inasmuch as ye were born into the world by water, and blood, and the spirit, which I have made, and so became of dust a living soul, even so ye must be born again into the kingdom of heaven, of water, and of the Spirit, and be cleansed by blood, even the blood of mine Only Begotten; that ye might be sanctified from all sin, and enjoy the words of eternal life in this world, and eternal life in the world to come, even immortal glory; (Moses 6:59)

The way we allow the leaven to spread throughout us, or the graft to change the kind of fruit we produce, is to seek and hearked to the word of God. The process progresses to the degree that we seek and accept his word. The more we accept and do, the more we get:

> And therefore, he that will harden his heart, the same receiveth the lesser portion of the word; and he that will not harden his heart, to him is given the greater portion of the word, until it is given unto him to know

the mysteries of God until he know them in full. (Alma
12:10)

This process occurs as individuals seek and declare the word of
God: "And Alma went forth, and also Amulek, among the people,
to declare the words of God unto them; and they were filled
with the Holy Ghost."[19] The Lord himself followed this process
during his mortal ministry. Being born as devoid of God's word
as any man,[20] he followed the word he received line upon line and
precept upon precept until it could be said of him: "For he whom
God hath sent speaketh the words of God: for God giveth not the
Spirit by measure unto him."[21] Those who faithfully seek, obtain,
and heed God's word will be visited by the Father and the Son:

> Jesus answered and said unto him, If a man love me,
> he will keep my words: and my Father will love him,
> and we will come unto him, and make our abode with
> him. (John 14:23)

Though this scripture indicates a physical visit from these two
beings, it also conveys the sanctification process that occurs as the
mind and will of God, which is a fullness of his word, become
infused in his spirit. This enables him to say, as did Jesus, that he
is in the Father, and the Father in him.[22]

In order to achieve Zion, the word must be found in us. We
have to have become like God. Thus, "when he shall appear, we

---

[19] Alma 8:30
[20] "And he received not of the fulness at first, but continued
from grace to grace, until he received a fulness;" (D&C 93:13)
[21] John 3:34
[22] John 14:10

shall be like him; for we shall see him as he is."[23] The lack of seeking, heeding, and living God's word is cited by God as the reason that Zion has not yet come again.

> *...when men should keep all my commandments*, Zion should again come on the earth, the city of Enoch which I have caught up unto myself. And this is mine everlasting covenant, that when thy posterity shall embrace the truth, and look upward, then shall Zion look downward, and all the heavens shall shake with gladness, and the earth shall tremble with joy; And the general assembly of the church of the firstborn shall come down out of heaven, and possess the earth, and shall have place until the end come. And this is mine everlasting covenant, which I made with thy father Enoch. (JST Gen 9:21-23)

Rejecting God's word, which includes not seeking it in the first place, brings penalties. The most harmful of these is that, while embracing God's word makes our spirits (and by association, our flesh) holy, rejecting it "quenches" that connection with God, severing us from his sanctifying process.

> Behold, will ye reject these words? Will ye reject the words of the prophets; and will ye reject all the words which have been spoken concerning Christ, after so many have spoken concerning him; and deny the good word of Christ, and the power of God, and the gift of

---

[23] 1 John 3:2

the Holy Ghost, and quench the Holy Spirit, and make a mock of the great plan of redemption, which hath been laid for you? (Jacob 6:8)

Those who reject God's word lose the light and truth that they previously acquired, until the spirit of God is not found at all within them.[24] We see that those who are in this state of spiritual atrophy are capable of the grossest sin. King Noah, for example, not only rejected a true messenger of God, but murdered him by fire.[25] Jesus said that the reason that some sought to kill him was that his word was not found in them. "I know that ye are Abraham's seed; but ye seek to kill me, because my word hath no place in you."[26] Thus Alma tells us that

if our hearts have been hardened, yea, if we have hardened our hearts against the word, insomuch that it has not been found in us, then will our state be awful, for then we shall be condemned. (Alma 12:13)

The sheep hear the voice of the true shepard. However, if the word does not abide in us:

- We will not recognize true messengers: "And ye have not his word abiding in you: for whom he hath sent, him ye believe

---

[24] See Alma 12:10

[25] "Now the eyes of the people were blinded; therefore they hardened their hearts against the words of Abinadi, and they sought from that time forward to take him. And king Noah hardened his heart against the word of the Lord, and he did not repent of his evil doings." (Mosiah 11:29)

[26] John 8:37

not."[27]

- We will not understand the scriptures: "Why do ye not understand my speech? even because ye cannot hear my word."[28]

- We will not hear the voice of the Spirit to us: "He that is of God heareth God's words: ye therefore hear them not, because ye are not of God."[29]

- We will not heed the word of God: "Now Satan had gotten great hold upon the hearts of the people of the city of Ammonihah; therefore they would not hearken unto the words of Alma."[30]

The word may not abide in us because we do not seek it. Perhaps it does not abide in us because we have replaced his word with the words of men, or some other idol. Maybe it has fled from us because we have refused to heed it. Sometimes, we avoid God's word because we know we are acting contrary to the light and truth we have received, and we do not trust that he knows better than us what will bring us happiness:

> And this is the condemnation, that light is come into the world, and men loved darkness rather than light, because their deeds were evil. For every one that doeth evil hateth the light, neither cometh to the light, lest

[27]John 5:38
[28]John 8:43
[29]John 8:47
[30]Alma 8:9

his deeds should be reproved. But he that doeth truth cometh to the light, that his deeds may be made manifest, that they are wrought in God. (John 3:19-21)

When we do seek and heed the word of God, we can count on several things:

- We will see God's hand in their life: "And thus the work of the Lord did commence among the Lamanites; thus the Lord did begin to pour out his Spirit upon them; and we see that his arm is extended to all people who will repent and believe on his name."[31]

- We will be asked to do hard things.[32]

---

[31]Alma 19:36

[32]"Let us here observe, that a religion that does not require the sacrifice of all things, never has power sufficient to produce the faith necessary unto life and salvation; for from the first existence of man, the faith necessary unto the enjoyment of life and salvation never could be obtained without the sacrifice of all earthly things; it was through this sacrifice, and this only, that God has ordained that men should enjoy eternal life; and it is through the medium of the sacrifice of all earthly things, that men do actually know that they are doing the things that are well pleasing in the sight of God. When a man has offered in sacrifice all that he has for the truth's sake, not even withholding his life, and believing before God that he has been called to make this sacrifice, because he seeks to do his will, he does know most assuredly that God does and will accept his sacrifice and overing, and that he has not nor will not seek his face in vain. Under these circumstances then, he can obtain the faith necessary for him to lay hold on eternal life. (Lectures on Faith 6:7)

- We will work miracles in God's name: "And there were great and marvelous works wrought by the disciples of Jesus, insomuch that they did heal the sick, and raise the dead, and cause the lame to walk, and the blind to receive their sight, and the deaf to hear; and all manner of miracles did they work among the children of men; and in nothing did they work miracles save it were in the name of Jesus."[33]

- We will have power in their preaching: "And as Enoch spake forth the words of God, the people trembled, and could not stand in his presence."[34]

- We will be hated by the world: "I have given them thy word; and the world hath hated them, because they are not of the world, even as I am not of the world."[35]

We need to let God's word "sink down into [our] ears."[36] We need to obey God's command to cleave to his word: "And I give unto you a commandment, that ye shall forsake all evil and cleave unto all good, that ye shall live by every word which proceedeth forth out of the mouth of God."[37] When we do so, we will find the words of eternal life in ourselves.

---

[33] 4 Nephi 1:5
[34] Moses 6:47
[35] John 17:14
[36] Luke 9:44
[37] D&C 98:11

The Two-Edged Sword

"...and out of his mouth went a sharp twoedged
sword..."

–Revelation 1:16

John the Revelator described Jesus saying that "out of his
mouth went a sharp twoedged sword...".[1] This is the same message
that is conveyed in D&C 6:2, D&C 11:2, D&C 12:2, and D&C
14:2. In each case, the verse reads: "Behold, I am God; give heed
to my word, which is quick and powerful, sharper than a twoedged sword, to the dividing asunder of both joints and marrow;
therefore give heed unto my word." Why do you suppose that
God would repeat himself so many times? Could it be that the
object of the analogy—the word of God—is important enough to
justify it?

Imagine yourself as one of the mighty and noble ones shown to
Abraham. You have already proven yourself to God and obtained
glory with him. Yet, you willingly offer to condescend to a filthy,

---

[1]Revelation 1:16

polluted place, completely outnumbered. You know fully that you will be almost utterly rejected. You realize the tremendous effort that will be required to save a few souls. This is tantamount to accepting a search and rescue mission behind enemy lines knowing full well that your whole team will probably die, on the outside chance that you might be able to rescue one or two captives. Were you to accept such a mission, what weapon would you choose?

Mormon makes clear the weapon he would choose. As he abridged the record of Alma he wrote,

> And now, as the preaching of the word had a great tendency to lead the people to do that which was just—yea, it had had more powerful effect upon the minds of the people than the sword, or anything else, which had happened unto them—therefore Alma thought it was expedient that they should try the virtue of the word of God. (Alma 31:5)

Mormon's choice of weapon is the word of God. While Christ himself had greater force than any earthly army within his arsenal, he instead opted to use persuasion, long-suffering, gentleness, meekness, love unfeigned, kindness, and pure knowledge.[2] Jesus does not employ speculation, opinion, force, compulsion, dominion, arrogance, or arbitrary threats. His word is the vehicle for

---

[2] "No power or influence can or ought to be maintained by virtue of the priesthood, only by persuasion, by long-suffering, by gentleness and meekness, and by love unfeigned; By kindness, and pure knowledge, which shall greatly enlarge the soul without hypocrisy, and without guile." (D&C 121:41-42)

these attributes. By his word we learn of his attributes. By his word they are demonstrated.

This weapon is available to all of us. When we seek and heed the word of God, it acts on us. When we obtain it and then provide it to others, it acts on them.

> Yea, we see that whosoever will may lay hold upon the word of God, which is quick and powerful, which shall divide asunder all the cunning and the snares and the wiles of the devil, and lead the man of Christ in a strait and narrow course across that everlasting gulf of misery which is prepared to engulf the wicked. (Helaman 3:29)

God's word in the Book of Mormon clearly teach us that it (his word) is the only foundation for salvation.

> And now, my sons, remember, remember that it is upon the rock of our Redeemer, who is Christ, the Son of God, that ye must build your foundation; that when the devil shall send forth his mighty winds, yea, his shafts in the whirlwind, yea, when all his hail and his mighty storm shall beat upon you, it shall have no power over you to drag you down to the gulf of misery and endless wo, because of the rock upon which ye are built, which is a sure foundation, a foundation whereon if men build they cannot fall. (Helaman 5:12)

Despite the plainness of this instruction, many have or will face the disappointment and pain that always eventually comes to those

159

who set up a foundation on sand. The promise for peace lies only in building our foundation upon the rock. What is the rock?

> And I said unto them that it was the word of God; and whoso would hearken unto the word of God, and would hold fast unto it, they would never perish; neither could the temptations and the fiery darts of the adversary overpower them unto blindness, to lead them away to destruction. (1 Nephi 15:24)

It is the word of God. As Nephi said, this only includes secondary sources when those sources are explicit repetitions from heaven: "Cursed is he that putteth his trust in man, or maketh flesh his arm, or shall hearken unto the precepts of men, save their precepts shall be given by the power of the Holy Ghost."[3] This doctrine offends many, but it ought not be offensive. After all,

> ...we talk of Christ, we rejoice in Christ, we preach of Christ, we prophesy of Christ, and we write according to our prophecies, that our children may know to what source they may look for a remission of their sins. (2 Nephi 25:26)

Jacob's quoted allegory of the olive tree mentions branches whose loftiness exceeded the root.

> And it came to pass that the servant said unto his master: Is it not the loftiness of thy vineyard—have not the branches thereof overcome the roots which

---

[3] 2 Nephi 28:31

are good? And because the branches have overcome the roots thereof, behold they grew faster than the strength of the roots, taking strength unto themselves. Behold, I say, is not this the cause that the trees of thy vineyard have become corrupted? (Jacob 5:48)

This was a common occurrence in Israel. However, if we are connected directly to the root, and we don't rely on the branches to bring us nourishment of the pure word of Christ, these corruptions cannot harm us. We can have fellow Christians who let us down, we can have leaders who offend us, we can experience numberless doctrinal errors professed by our friends, and the word of God is still true. When we separate the foundation from the superstructure, the root from the branches, we are only susceptible to our own failings, not those of others.

Interestingly, Nephi criticized those who, in our day, would say they don't want any more truth. "And in fine, wo unto all those who tremble, and are angry because of the truth of God! For behold, he that is built upon the rock receiveth it with gladness; and he that is built upon a sandy foundation trembleth lest he shall fall." (2 Nephi 28:28) The weakness of a sandy foundation is not apparent until the quake or the rains hit. Yet Christ explicitly commanded us not to establish foundations on sand:

And whoso shall declare more or less than this, and establish it for my doctrine, the same cometh of evil, and is not built upon my rock; but he buildeth upon a sandy foundation, and the gates of hell stand open to receive such when the floods come and the winds beat upon them. (3 Nephi 11:40)

The word of God always—ALWAYS—leads us to Christ. This is the sum of the subject: obtain the word of God and live it. If you do, you will build your foundation on the rock.

> And now, my beloved brethren, and also Jew, and all ye ends of the earth, hearken unto these words and believe in Christ; and if ye believe not in these words believe in Christ. And if ye shall believe in Christ ye will believe in these words, for they are the words of Christ, and he hath given them unto me; and they teach all men that they should do good. (2 Nephi 33:10)

Made in the USA
San Bernardino, CA
02 June 2016